BIG
BUY
COOKING

BIG BUY COOKING

THE FOOD LOVER'S GUIDE TO
BUYING IN BULK
AND USING IT ALL UP

From the Editors of Fine Cooking

Huntington City
Township Public Library
255 West Park Drive
Huntington, IN 46750

The Taunton Press

The Taunton Press
Inspiration for hands-on living®

The Taunton Press, Inc.,
63 South Main Street,
PO Box 5506,
Newtown, CT 06470-5506
e-mail: tp@taunton.com

Editor: Courtney Jordan
Copy editor: W. Anne Jones
Indexer: Heidi Blough
Interior design: Stark Design
Layout: Catherine Cassidy
Photographer: Maren Caruso, except
  photo (bottom center) on front cover
  by Scott Phillips, courtesy Fine Cooking,
  © The Taunton Press, Inc.
Food stylist: Katie Christ
Recipe tester: Claudia Nachemson
Recipe developer: Tony Rosenfeld except for
  recipes on pp. 53–56, 91–94, which were
  developed by Allison Ehri Kreitler.

Fine Cooking® is a trademark of The Taunton Press, Inc.,
  registered in the U.S. Patent and Trademark Office.

Library of Congress Cataloging-in-Publication Data

Big buy : the food lovers guide to buying in bulk and using it all up / editors of Fine cooking
     p. cm.
  ISBN 978-1-60085-154-4
  1. Cookery. 2. Grocery shopping. I. Fine cooking.
  TX714.B542 2010
  640.73--dc22

                        2009046116

Printed in the United States of America
10 9 8 7 6 5 4 3 2 1

The following names/manufacturers appearing in Big Buy Cooking are trademarks:
Cryovac®, Grand Marnier®, Lee Kum Kee™, Pernod®, Quaker®, Tabasco®

CONTENTS

INTRODUCTION

I've never known a food lover who didn't jump at the idea of a trip to a warehouse store. Sure, we're all big on farmer's markets, specialty food stores, ethnic markets, bakeries, and health food stores, but there's something irresistible about the prospect of an hour (or three) spent trolling the aisles of a big box store. Call it the thrill of the hunt. Since the selection changes often and with the seasons, you're always guaranteed to find new products and produce. Who knows what amazing thing you might turn up?

Every cook's favorite brand of canned tomatoes, to begin with, along with some excellent cheeses (Grana Padano, feta, and a very good white cheddar, to name just three) are at your fingertips. Sun-dried tomatoes and Kalamata olives, pine nuts, capers, sausages, and richly marbled steaks make the trip worth it. And that's just a start. Good cooks know: The warehouse stores (along with some of the markets that now carry bulk buys) are stocked with top-notch finds at bargain-basement prices.

Of course when you let a cook loose in a place like that, with all those options at low, low prices, you can guess what's going to happen: We're going to fill that outsized grocery cart with more food than any single family can consume in the space of a week. That flat of blueberries looked far too gorgeous to pass up; that side of salmon had "great barbecue" written all over it; and that big bag of avocados sang out to the guacamole lover in you. In the end, we haul our treasures home, unload the bounty, and begin the process of trying to find refrigerator/cupboard/garage space for it. That's when the niggling worry sets in: How on earth are we going to use it all up?

That's also where this book comes in. It's packed with great recipes for doing just that: using it all up. All those roasted red peppers, those beautiful haricots verts, those perfectly ripe mangos. As we see it, buying in bulk offers an opportunity to get cooking, to celebrate the many delicious possibilities in any of the big buys you simply can't not buy.

Take that wheel of brie. You probably would have passed it by if you'd seen it at your local market, where it might have been on the costly side and perhaps a little long in the tooth. Not the one at the big box store: It's cheap, ripe, and calling out to you. Go on, give in. Once home, cut yourself a wedge to enjoy with grapes and crackers, and then let the cooking begin. Brie on crostini, warm and melting, with dates and walnuts. Brie, ham, and tart apples on a toasted baguette, with a hit of Dijon mustard and honey. Brie in the best-ever version of fondue.

And what about that big bag of multicolored fingerling potatoes, another ingredient you might not buy elsewhere, if only for the typically steep cost? Not at the big box store. Don't ask why, just buy, and then try them pan-fried (with some Southwest seasonings); in a warm salad (with red-wine vinegar and chives); and roasted (with shallots and fresh rosemary). Grill some steaks (you did buy that six-pack of New York strips, we're assuming) to go with any of these options, and dinner's on the table.

This book takes its inspiration from a regular column in *Fine Cooking* magazine, where the conversation about what to cook with who's-bought-what is an everyday topic. Each issue of the magazine features one of our latest Big Buys, with creative recipes for using it up. And on our website, finecooking.com, we're keeping the ideas coming—and hoping that you'll join the party, too, and share your ideas and discoveries and recipes. The more, the merrier—and the more reasons we have to run on over and see what's new in the big buy aisles.

Laurie Buckle
Editor
Fine Cooking

PANTRY

With an unmistakably rich color and briny taste, Kalamatas are a cut above canned black olives. They're usually pricey, but buying them in bulk gives you the opportunity to indulge without sticker shock.

KALAMATA OLIVES

BLACK OLIVE
& ROSEMARY VINAIGRETTE

Olives add depth of flavor and a rich, dark color to this vinaigrette. Pair the dressing with the components of a Greek salad—tomatoes, cucumbers, feta, and Romaine—or with a hearty spinach salad of goat cheese, roasted root vegetables, and baby spinach.

Makes about 1½ cups

1 cup pitted Kalamata olives, coarsely chopped

¼ cup fresh lemon juice

1 teaspoon Dijon mustard

1 small clove garlic, minced and mashed to a paste

¾ cup extra-virgin olive oil

1½ teaspoons chopped fresh rosemary

Freshly ground black pepper

Put the olives, lemon juice, mustard, and garlic in a food processor or blender and purée. With the machine running, add the oil in a thin steady stream so the mixture becomes uniform and thick, and then add the rosemary and 1 teaspoon pepper. Add 2 to 3 tablespoons of water to thin the vinaigrette to a pourable consistency if needed. Use immediately or store in an airtight container in the refrigerator for up to one week.

PITTING OLIVES

There are all sorts of fancy gadgets you can buy to pit olives. And while many of them work just fine, the most efficient tools for the task just might be your own two hands. Set the heel of one of your hands (the pad right near the thumb) over an olive and press down with just a bit of weight. The flesh of the olive will splinter and you will easily be able to pick out the pit.

prep this

SWORDFISH WITH BLACK OLIVE & MINT TAPENADE

Make a double batch of this versatile black olive paste and use the extra as a dressing for pasta, sandwiches, or sautés, or as a garnish for grilled or roasted chicken. It's paired with fish here, so anchovies (an ingredient in traditional tapenade) are omitted, but feel free to add them if you like.

Serves 4

FOR THE TAPENADE
1 cup pitted Kalamata olives,
  coarsely chopped
2 oil-packed sun-dried tomatoes, chopped
2 tablespoons extra-virgin olive oil
8 basil leaves, torn into small pieces
2 tablespoons coarsely chopped fresh mint
1 medium clove garlic, minced and mashed
  to a paste
Large pinch crushed red pepper flakes

FOR THE SWORDFISH
Four 1-inch-thick swordfish fillets
  (6 to 7 ounces each)
Coarsely cracked black pepper
Kosher salt
1 tablespoon olive oil

FOR SERVING
1 pint ripe grape or cherry tomatoes, halved
2 tablespoons chopped fresh mint
2 tablespoons extra-virgin olive oil
Kosher salt

MAKE THE TAPENADE
Put the olives, sun-dried tomatoes, and oil in a food processor and pulse until the mixture forms a coarse paste. Pulse in the basil, mint, garlic, and red pepper flakes until combined and transfer to a medium bowl.

MAKE THE SWORDFISH
Heat a gas grill to medium high, or prepare a medium-hot charcoal fire. Clean and oil the grates to prevent sticking. Sprinkle the fish with 1 teaspoon pepper and $\frac{1}{2}$ teaspoon salt and drizzle with oil. Grill the fish until it has good grill marks, about 4 minutes. Using both tongs and a spatula, carefully turn the fish. Continue cooking until the other side has good grill marks and the fish is just cooked through, about 8 minutes.

TO SERVE
Toss the tomatoes with the mint, oil, and $\frac{1}{2}$ teaspoon salt. Transfer the fish to a platter, spread generously with the tapenade, and top with a spoonful of the tomatoes (and their juices). Serve immediately.

 MAKE IT LAST Canned or jarred olives will keep indefinitely in your pantry. Once opened, refrigerate a jar of brined olives (in their brine) in the refrigerator for up to one month. If you buy olives from your deli, try to use them within one week.

SPICY PENNE TOSSED WITH CHICKEN, BROCCOLI & CHOPPED OLIVES

Kalamata olives enhance any dish with their salty, rich flavor. Here, they add a twist to a basic chicken and broccoli pasta. For a vegetarian option, omit the chicken and add red and green peppers, garbanzo beans, or any other legume or vegetable of your choice when the pasta and pasta water is added to the skillet.

Serves 4 to 6

Kosher salt

½ cup olive oil

4 cloves garlic, smashed

2 teaspoons chopped fresh rosemary

½ teaspoon crushed red pepper flakes

½ pound (about 1 large) boneless, skinless chicken breast, cut into thin strips

⅔ cup pitted Kalamata olives, coarsely chopped

1 pound penne

½ pound broccoli florets, cut into 1½-inch pieces (about 3 cups)

2 tablespoons fresh lemon juice

1 cup freshly grated Pecorino-Romano

Bring a large pot of well-salted water to a boil over high heat. Meanwhile, heat the oil and garlic in a 12-inch skillet over medium heat, stirring gently so the cloves don't break up, until they become light brown in places and very fragrant, 2 to 3 minutes. Add the rosemary and red pepper flakes and cook until they start to sizzle, about 15 seconds. Add the chicken, sprinkle with ¼ teaspoon salt, and cook, stirring often, until the chicken loses its raw color, about 2 minutes. Remove from the heat and stir in the olives.

Add the penne to the boiling water and cook, stirring occasionally, until just barely al dente, 1 to 2 minutes less than the package instructions. Add the broccoli and cook until it turns bright green and the pasta is tender, about 1 minute. Reserve ½ cup of the pasta water, and then drain the pasta and broccoli. Discard the garlic from the olive mixture. Add the pasta and the pasta water to the skillet and cook uncovered over medium-high heat, stirring, until the pasta absorbs most of the liquid, about 2 minutes. Stir in the lemon juice and half of the Pecorino. Serve sprinkled with the remaining Pecorino.

Most big buy stores carry fresh-baked artisan breads, often in two-packs. Make some great sandwiches and then venture into new bread territory with these imaginative recipes.

BREAD

WARM MAPLE & CINNAMON
BREAD PUDDING

Take the flavors of a coffee cake, apply them to a bread pudding, and you get this warming custard, reminiscent of French toast and perfect for brunch or dessert. For the best results, let the custard soak into the bread for at least 4 hours before baking.

Serves 8 to 10

Unsalted butter for the pan

3 cups whole milk

8 large eggs, beaten

1 teaspoon pure vanilla extract

Kosher salt

1 cup walnuts (about 4 ounces), toasted (see Toasting Nuts, p. 41)

½ cup light brown sugar

1 teaspoon ground cinnamon

1 pound rustic white bread (like ciabatta), cut into ¾-inch-thick slices

¾ cup pure maple syrup

Confectioners' sugar for sprinkling (optional)

To assemble the bread pudding, butter a 9x13-inch baking dish. In a medium bowl, whisk the milk with the eggs, vanilla, and ¾ teaspoon salt. In a mini chopper or food processor, pulse the walnuts with the brown sugar and cinnamon. Arrange half the bread slices in an even layer on the bottom of the dish; cut slices into small pieces to fill in the holes. Cover with half of the egg mixture, a third of the nuts, and a third of the maple syrup. Make another layer with the remaining bread and cover with the rest of the egg mixture, another third of the nuts, and a third of the maple syrup. Sprinkle with the rest of the nut mixture and maple syrup. Cover with plastic wrap, pressing down so the bread is completely submerged in the egg mixture, and refrigerate for at least 4 hours and up to 2 days before baking.

Position a rack in the center of the oven and heat the oven to 350°F. Let the bread pudding sit at room temperature while the oven heats. Bake until the custard starts to set, about 30 minutes. Loosely cover the pudding with foil to prevent browning, and cook for another 10 minutes. Let cool for 10 minutes and serve sprinkled with the confectioners' sugar, if desired.

continued

VARIATION

To make individual bread puddings, butter eight 10-ounce ramekins and fill each halfway with a layer of bread and cover with 1/8 cup of the egg mixture. Sprinkle with the nuts and 1 teaspoon maple syrup. Repeat with a second layer of bread and egg mixture, nuts, and syrup; the ramekins should be about three-quarters full. Cover each ramekin with plastic wrap, pressing down so that the bread is submerged in the egg mixture, and refrigerate for at least 4 hours. When ready to bake, put the ramekins on a large rimmed baking sheet lined with parchment paper and bake in the center of a 350°F oven. Start checking for doneness after 30 minutes.

 MAKE IT LAST It's perfectly fine to use stale bread for the bread recipes in this book, but, of course, you don't want to use it if it's moldy. Whole grain and wheat breads are more susceptible to mold than white breads, so slice and freeze them to hold for cooking. Most rustic white breads will keep fine at room temperature for four or five days in a cool, dry cupboard. If you decide to turn the bread into breadcrumbs, store those in a zip-top bag or airtight container in the freezer.

left: warm maple & cinnamon **bread pudding**

GRILLED BREAD SALAD
WITH BASIL & CHERRY TOMATOES

A trip to the grill gives the makings of a classic Italian bread salad—a good crusty loaf of bread, ripe summer tomatoes, and basil—a little smokiness and crisp texture. Because this salad can sit out at room temperature for an hour or two, it's the perfect side for a picnic or barbecue. If you can't find bocconcini—small fresh mozzarella balls—substitute a large fresh mozzarella cut into 1-inch pieces.

Serves 8

1 medium loaf (about ½ pound) rustic white bread (like ciabatta), cut lengthwise into 1-inch-thick slices
½ cup extra-virgin olive oil
Kosher salt
1 clove garlic, halved lengthwise
1 pint cherry or grape tomatoes, halved
1 bunch scallions (about 8), trimmed and thinly sliced (both white and green parts)
12 large basil leaves, torn into small pieces
¼ cup red-wine vinegar
8 ounces fresh bocconcini, halved

Prepare a medium-high fire on a gas or charcoal grill. Clean and oil the grates to prevent sticking. Using a pastry brush, dab both sides of the bread slices with 2 tablespoons oil and sprinkle with ½ teaspoon salt. Grill the bread until it browns and gets good grill marks, about 2 minutes.

Grill the other side until browned, about 2 minutes, and transfer to a large cutting board to cool. Rub the cut sides of the garlic over the bread and discard the garlic. Put the cherry tomatoes and scallions in a large serving bowl with the basil. Cut the bread into 1-inch pieces and add to the bowl.

In a small bowl, whisk the remaining oil with the red-wine vinegar, pour over the bread mixture, and toss well. Let the salad sit for up to 2 hours before serving. Just before serving, fold in the bocconcini and season with salt to taste.

LOAFING IT

The peasant cuisines of the Mediterranean were based on making meals out of the leftovers at hand. Bread was often in ample supply and formed the base for many dishes. Follow the lead of southern Italian cooks and make breadcrumbs from stale loaves to sprinkle on pastas and soups. They add a crisp texture and a pleasant nutty flavor. Leftover bread also goes great in soups like Spanish gazpacho (see our take on this chilled soup, Chilled Red Pepper Soup with Sautéed Shrimp, on p. 39), Tuscan Pappa al Pomodoro (a spicy tomato and bread soup), or as a crouton topper for French onion soup.

ASPARAGUS, HAM & MUSHROOM STRATA

A strata is like an Italian quiche, but instead of an involved pastry crust, leftover bread forms the egg custard base. As with a bread pudding, assemble this dish ahead of time and bake it just before serving. It's up to you whether or not to trim the bread crust. When entertaining, trim it for a neat and pretty dish or leave it intact for a heartier texture.

Serves 8

2 tablespoons unsalted butter, more for the pan

1 pound asparagus, ends snapped off, cut into 1½-inch pieces

Kosher salt and freshly ground black pepper

3½ ounces oyster mushrooms (or shiitake or white mushrooms), stemmed and thinly sliced

6 scallions, trimmed and thinly sliced, white and green parts separated (½ cup green, 2 tablespoons white)

9 large eggs, beaten

2¾ cups milk (preferably whole)

1 large loaf (about 1 pound) rustic white bread (like ciabatta), cut into 1-inch cubes

8 ounces thinly sliced deli ham, cut into 1-inch strips

3 cups grated extra sharp Cheddar (about 8 ounces)

Melt the butter in a large (12-inch) skillet over medium-high heat. Add the asparagus, sprinkle with ½ teaspoon each salt and pepper, and cook, stirring occasionally, until the spears start to brown and soften, about 3 minutes. Add the mushrooms and scallion whites and cook, stirring occasionally, until the mushrooms soften and cook through, about 2 minutes. Remove from the heat and let cool for a couple of minutes.

Butter a 9x13-inch baking dish. Whisk the eggs with the milk and ½ teaspoon each salt and pepper. Spread half the bread in a single layer on the bottom of the baking dish. Top with half the egg mixture and then cover with half the ham, cheese, and asparagus mixture, and sprinkle with half the scallion greens. Repeat with the remaining custard, ham, cheese, asparagus mixture, and scallions. Cover with plastic wrap, pressing down so the bread is completely submerged in the egg mixture, and refrigerate for at least 4 hours and up to 2 days before baking.

Put a rack in the center of the oven and heat the oven to 350°F. Let the strata sit at room temperature while the oven heats. Bake until the custard sets and the top browns, about 30 minutes. Loosely cover with foil and bake for another 20 minutes. Let cool for 10 minutes, cut into square pieces, and serve.

Canned tomatoes are a great pantry staple, no matter the season. And the big buy stores often carry the best brands at a real savings.

CANNED TOMATOES

QUICK MARINARA
WITH TOASTED GARLIC & ROSEMARY

There's no need to open a jar of sauce when you can whisk this homemade creation together in the time it takes to cook a pot of pasta. This is a large batch, so use the extra as a base for stews, pizzas, and sautés. It will also keep in the freezer for at least three months.

Makes about 5½ cups of sauce

Two 28-ounce cans plum tomatoes with their juices (6 cups) (preferably San Marzano)
3 tablespoons olive oil
3 medium cloves garlic, chopped
1 teaspoon chopped fresh rosemary
¼ teaspoon crushed red pepper flakes
Kosher salt and freshly ground black pepper
1 teaspoon granulated sugar (optional)

Strain off and discard ½ cup of the tomatoes' juices (this will give the sauce a thicker consistency). Heat the oil and garlic in a 4-quart saucepan over medium heat until the garlic sizzles steadily and turns golden brown in places, about 3 minutes. Add the rosemary and red pepper flakes; reduce the heat to medium low, and cook, stirring, for 30 seconds. Add the tomatoes and their remaining juices, 1 teaspoon salt, and ½ teaspoon pepper, and bring to a boil. Reduce to a gentle simmer, cover with the lid ajar, and cook for 15 minutes, stirring occasionally, so the flavors meld and the sauce reduces slightly. Using an immersion blender or working in batches in a regular blender, purée the sauce. Taste the sauce and season with more salt, pepper, or red pepper flakes if needed. If too acidic, add the sugar. Serve immediately or let cool to room temperature and refrigerate for up to one week, or freeze in zip-top bags or airtight containers.

VARIATION
For a spicy tomato-vodka sauce, add 3 tablespoons vodka with the tomatoes. After puréeing the sauce, stir in ¼ cup Parmigiano-Reggiano, ¼ cup chopped fresh flat-leaf parsley instead of rosemary, and 3 tablespoons heavy cream. Let the sauce simmer for 5 minutes. Serve over rigatoni, topped with more Parmigiano.

BRAISED BEEF BRACIOLA STUFFED WITH BASIL & MOZZARELLA

This is a home-style version of the Italian-American classic. The traditional dish uses small roulades of beef round, but here we use a whole flank steak because it's quicker and easier to stuff and roll one large cut and the flank offers a wonderful flavor. If you want to build up the stuffing, add prosciutto or hearty greens like kale.

Serves 6

One 2-pound flank steak
Kosher salt and freshly ground
    black pepper
1 cup grated mozzarella
¾ cup freshly grated
    Parmigiano-Reggiano
⅓ cup fine, dry breadcrumbs
12 large basil leaves, torn into pieces
¼ cup olive oil
1 large yellow onion, cut into thin strips
    (about 1½ cups)
½ cup red wine
One 28-ounce can whole tomatoes and
    their juices (3 cups), puréed
    (preferably San Marzano)
¼ teaspoon crushed red pepper flakes
8 ounces white mushrooms, quartered

Set the flank steak on a large cutting board. Using a chef's knife, slice the steak lengthwise along one long side (without cutting all the way through the meat) and open it up like a book. Using a meat mallet, flatten the meat so it is about ¼ inch thick. Sprinkle both sides of the meat with 1 teaspoon salt and ½ teaspoon pepper. For the stuffing, put the mozzarella, Parmigiano, breadcrumbs, and basil in a mini chopper or food processor and pulse to combine. Sprinkle the stuffing evenly over one side of the beef, and roll it up lengthwise jelly roll–style with the stuffing inside. Secure with kitchen twine in five or six places.

Heat half the oil in a large Dutch oven over medium-high heat until it's shimmering. Add the beef and cook until it browns and releases easily from the pan, about 2 minutes. Flip and cook the other side until browned, about 5 more minutes. Transfer to a large plate.

Add the remaining 2 tablespoons oil and the onion to the pan, and lower the heat to medium. Sprinkle with ½ teaspoon salt and cook, stirring, until the onion wilts completely and turns a light brown, about 8 minutes. Add the red wine and cook, stirring, until it almost completely reduces, about 2 minutes. Add the tomatoes and red pepper flakes and bring to a boil. Reduce to a gentle simmer and tuck the meat and mushrooms into the broth. Cover and cook, repositioning the meat occasionally, until the

meat becomes tender and cuts easily with a paring knife, about 1½ hours. Set the meat on a cutting board and let rest for 10 to 15 minutes. Thinly slice and serve topped with the sauce and vegetables.

WHOLE TOMATOES VS. TOMATO PURÉE
In most big buy stores and supermarkets, you're often presented with the option of whole tomatoes or crushed and peeled tomatoes. While you might think that buying crushed will save time in your cooking, go for the whole tomatoes. It's likely the whole tomatoes are of a higher quality than those used to make the can of crushed tomatoes. Regardless of what size can you buy, you'll find that whole tomatoes have a clean, nuanced flavor unlike the crushed peeled tomatoes, which can vary considerably in quality and flavor depending on the brand.

SMOKY TOMATO SOUP

A combination of bacon and smoked paprika gives this tomato soup a strong profile that goes perfectly with a gooey grilled cheese sandwich. Go with the sweet pimentón for a rich taste with little heat, or try the hot for a spicier kick in the soup.

Makes 4 cups

1 tablespoon olive oil

3 thick strips bacon (about 3 ounces), thinly sliced

1 large yellow onion, diced (about 1½ cups)

Kosher salt

1 tablespoon unbleached all-purpose flour

1 tablespoon chopped fresh thyme

½ teaspoon sweet or hot pimentón (smoked paprika)

One 28-ounce can whole tomatoes and their juices (3 cups) (preferably San Marzano)

2 cups lower-salt chicken broth

2 tablespoons heavy cream

Freshly ground black pepper

Put the oil in a large saucepan, add the bacon, and cook over medium heat, stirring occasionally, until the bacon renders most of its fat, about 5 minutes. Transfer the bacon to a plate lined with paper towels; let drain and cool, and then coarsely chop. Add the onion and ½ teaspoon salt to the pan and cook, stirring, until the onion softens and starts to brown lightly, about 5 minutes. Stir in the flour, 2 teaspoons thyme, and the pimentón, and cook, stirring, for 1 minute. Add the tomatoes and chicken broth, and bring to a boil. Reduce to a simmer, cover with the lid slightly ajar, and cook, stirring occasionally, until the mixture thickens and the flavors meld, about 20 minutes. Using an immersion blender or working in batches in a regular blender, purée the soup. Return the soup to the pan, stir in the cream, and bring to a boil. Taste and season with salt and pepper if needed, ladle the soup into serving bowls and serve sprinkled with the bacon pieces and the remaining thyme.

MAKE IT LAST Unopened canned tomatoes will keep for at least one year, if not far longer. Once opened, transfer them to an airtight plastic container and refrigerate for up to five days; store in a zip-top bag in the freezer for six to eight months.

CAPERS

The salty tang of capers adds a surprising zing to any dish. These little flower buds are categorized and sold by size, with nonpareil being the smallest and most desirable.

SMOKED SALMON &
CAPER SPREAD

Serve this dressy spread with toasted baguette rounds and a dry, fruity white wine like Riesling. It would also make a great appetizer atop slices of cucumber—just cut the cucumber rounds ½ inch thick and top with a dollop of the spread. For breakfast or brunch, serve with bagels or over scrambled eggs with slices of sweet, ripe melon like cantaloupe or honeydew on the side.

Serves 8

6 ounces thinly sliced cold-smoked salmon

¾ cup crème fraîche

4 ounces cream cheese, softened

1 teaspoon finely grated lemon zest

1 tablespoon fresh lemon juice

8 drops Tabasco

Freshly ground black pepper

3 tablespoons capers, rinsed, drained, patted dry, and chopped

3 tablespoons thinly sliced chives

In a food processor, combine the salmon, crème fraîche, cream cheese, lemon zest and juice, Tabasco®, and 1 teaspoon black pepper; process until just blended. Transfer to a large bowl and fold in the capers and chives. Taste and add more lemon juice or black pepper as desired. Serve immediately, or cover and refrigerate in an airtight container for up to one day; remove 15 minutes before serving to soften.

RINSING CAPERS

Whether you're using salt-cured capers or the more common brined capers, it's a good idea to give them a quick rinse before cooking. This washes off excess brine (or salt) and helps mellow the flavor. Pat them dry with paper towels after rinsing to absorb any excess liquid.

prep this

LEMON
CHICKEN BREASTS WITH
CAPERS

This sauté takes the traditional flavorings of chicken piccata and turns them outside-in. Boneless chicken breasts are stuffed with capers, lemon zest, and Parmesan. Breadcrumbs are added to help hold the mixture together.

Serves 4

4 boneless, skinless chicken breasts
(6 ounces each)

½ cup freshly grated Parmigiano-
Reggiano

¼ cup fine, dry breadcrumbs

4 tablespoons capers, rinsed, drained,
patted dry, and chopped

1 lemon, zest finely grated, and juiced

2 tablespoons chopped fresh flat-leaf
parsley

Kosher salt and freshly ground
black pepper

3 tablespoons unsalted butter

1 tablespoon olive oil

2 medium cloves garlic, thinly sliced

½ cup lower-salt chicken broth

MORE WAYS WITH CAPERS
Capers have a briny, sharp flavor that adds a savory edge to many dishes:
• Add to sauces and stews or beef sautés or sprinkle atop fish or grilled or roasted chicken.
• Capers are great in tomato-based pasta sauces and with seafood like scallops and tuna.
• Throw a handful into an egg salad, add them to omelets, and incorporate them into your favorite deviled egg recipe.
• Capers enhance any spread or mayonnaise.

Position a rack in the center of the oven and heat the oven to 425°F. Make a lengthwise horizontal slice almost all the way through each chicken breast and open each up like a book. Flatten the chicken with a meat mallet until it is ¼ inch thick. Put the Parmigiano, breadcrumbs, 3 tablespoons capers, lemon zest, and 1 tablespoon parsley in a mini chopper or food processor and pulse a few times to combine. Sprinkle the mixture on top of the chicken breasts. Fold each breast closed and secure with toothpicks. Sprinkle the breasts with ¾ teaspoon salt and ½ teaspoon pepper.

Heat 1 tablespoon butter and the oil in a large (12-inch), heavy-duty, oven-proof skillet over medium-high heat until the butter melts and starts to foam, about 2 minutes. Add the chicken and cook, without touching, until it browns and easily releases from the pan, about 2 minutes. Turn the chicken and cook the other side until browned, about 2 more minutes.

Add the garlic and the remaining tablespoon capers to the skillet, transfer the pan to the oven, and roast uncovered until the chicken cooks through (an instant-read thermometer inserted into the thickest part should register 165°F), about 8 minutes. Transfer the chicken to a serving platter and tent with foil.

Set the skillet over medium-high heat; add the chicken broth, and cook, scraping the bottom of the pan with a wooden spoon to loosen any browned bits, until it reduces

by about half, about 2 minutes. Remove from the heat and whisk in 2 tablespoons of the lemon juice and the remaining 2 tablespoons butter. Taste and add more lemon juice, salt, and pepper if needed. Serve the chicken drizzled with the butter sauce and sprinkled with the remaining tablespoon parsley.

 MAKE IT LAST Jarred capers will keep indefinitely in your pantry. Once opened, store them in their brine in an airtight container in the refrigerator. They will keep for at least six months.

SEARED STEAKS WITH CAPER-TARRAGON BUTTER

This easy, do-ahead caper butter is also good with roasted or grilled vegetables, like asparagus or red bell peppers. Wrapped in plastic, the butter will keep in the refrigerator for about a week.

Serves 4

½ cup unsalted butter, softened

3 tablespoons capers, rinsed, drained, patted dry, and chopped

2 tablespoons chopped fresh tarragon

1 small clove garlic, minced and mashed to a paste

½ teaspoon Worcestershire sauce

Kosher salt and freshly ground black pepper

Two 1-inch-thick boneless rib-eye steaks, each cut into 2 portions (6 to 8 ounces each)

2 tablespoons olive oil

In a medium bowl, mash the butter with the capers, tarragon, garlic, Worcestershire sauce, and ¼ teaspoon each salt and pepper. Spoon the mixture onto the center of a piece of plastic wrap and roll into a log, twisting and tightening the ends to secure them. Refrigerate for 1 hour to firm (the butter will keep for up to 2 days).

Set the steaks on a plate and sprinkle both sides with 1 teaspoon salt and 1 teaspoon coarsely ground black pepper. Let sit at room temperature for 15 to 30 minutes.

Heat the oil in a large (12-inch) heavy-duty skillet over medium-high heat until it's shimmering. Add the steaks, evenly spaced, and cook without touching until they brown nicely and easily release from the pan, about 3 minutes. Turn and cook the other sides in the same manner, 6 to 8 minutes for medium-rare (an instant-read thermometer inserted into the thickest part of the steak should read 135°F); see When It's Done for additional temperature guidelines for meat, p. 106.

To serve, place the steaks on a serving plate. Remove the butter from the refrigerator, thinly slice it, and top the steaks.

ROASTED RED PEPPERS

Jarred roasted red peppers deliver instant flavor without labor-intensive prep. Packed in oil, these smoky, sweet peppers add great color to any dish and are great for you.

SPICED COUSCOUS WITH FENNEL & ROASTED RED PEPPERS

Couscous is the culinary equivalent of a blank canvas. It soaks up and showcases whatever flavors—spicy, sweet, savory—are added to it. For our rendition, fennel serves as the aromatic base for this fragrant side dish.

Serves 4 to 6

3 tablespoons olive oil

1 medium bulb fennel, trimmed, cored, and cut into ½-inch dice (1½ cups)

Kosher salt

1 medium clove garlic, minced

2 teaspoons ground cumin

¼ teaspoon chipotle powder

¼ teaspoon ground cinnamon

2 jarred roasted red peppers, cut into ½-inch dice (1¼ cups)

1½ cups lower-salt chicken broth

1½ cups couscous

3 tablespoons coarsely chopped fresh cilantro

Heat the oil in a medium saucepan over medium-high heat. Add the fennel, sprinkle with ¾ teaspoon salt, and cook, stirring, until the fennel starts to brown and soften, about 4 minutes. Add the garlic and cook, stirring, until it becomes fragrant, about 30 seconds. Add the cumin, chipotle powder, and cinnamon; cook, stirring, for 30 seconds until the spices become fragrant. Add the red peppers and chicken broth, and bring to a boil. Stir in the couscous, remove from the heat, cover, and let sit until the liquid is absorbed; check after 5 minutes. Fluff the couscous with a fork and stir in the cilantro. Taste the couscous and season with salt as needed; serve immediately.

GARLICKY CHICKEN THIGHS IN RED PEPPER SAUCE

The main flavors in this one-pan dish—roasted red peppers, thyme, garlic, and sherry vinegar—are quintessentially Spanish. Sear the thighs on the stovetop to crisp the skin and then finish them in the oven to cook evenly.

Serves 4

2 tablespoons olive oil

8 bone-in skin-on chicken thighs (about 3 pounds), trimmed of excess fat and skin

Kosher salt and freshly ground black pepper

6 cloves garlic, smashed

2 teaspoons fresh thyme leaves

1 cup lower-salt chicken broth

3 jarred roasted red peppers, drained and cut into 1-inch strips (1½ cups)

1 medium russet potato, peeled and cut into ¾-inch dice (1½ cups)

1 tablespoon sherry vinegar

Crusty baguette for serving

Position a rack in the center of the oven and heat the oven to 425°F. Heat the oil in a large, oven-proof sauté pan over medium-high heat until it's shimmering. Sprinkle the chicken with 1½ teaspoons salt and ½ teaspoon pepper. Add half the thighs to the pan, skin side down. Reduce the heat to medium, and cook without touching until the skin browns and easily releases from the pan, about 3 minutes. Turn and cook for 1 minute. Transfer to a large plate. Add the remaining chicken and cook it in the same manner. Transfer the chicken to the plate. Add the garlic and thyme to the pan and cook until the garlic is lightly browned, 2 to 3 minutes. Add the chicken broth, red peppers, potato, and sherry vinegar to the pan, and bring to a boil. Remove from the heat, return the chicken to the pan skin side up, and transfer to the oven.

Braise the chicken, uncovered, until the potato pieces are tender and the chicken is completely cooked through, about 30 minutes. Serve with the baguette for soaking up the broth.

CHILLED RED PEPPER SOUP
WITH SAUTÉED SHRIMP

This cold soup builds on the flavors of Spanish gazpacho, only roasted red peppers take the place of tomatoes in the lead role.

Makes 6 cups

1 seedless English cucumber,
  peeled and roughly chopped

3 jarred roasted red peppers, cut into
  ½-inch dice (about 1½ cups)

3 cups tomato juice

2 slices baguette, toasted and cut into
  1-inch cubes (about 1 cup)

½ cup extra-virgin olive oil

2 tablespoons plus 1 teaspoon sherry
  vinegar or cider vinegar

1 medium clove garlic, minced
  and mashed to a paste

½ teaspoon ground cumin

Kosher salt and freshly ground
  black pepper

¾ pound medium shrimp
  (36 to 40 per pound), peeled and
  deveined

1 teaspoon chopped fresh thyme

Cut three-quarters of the cucumber into 1-inch pieces and purée in a blender with the red peppers, tomato juice, toasted bread, 6 tablespoons olive oil, 2 tablespoons vinegar, garlic, cumin, and ½ teaspoon each salt and pepper (you may have to purée the soup in batches, depending on the size of your blender). Taste and season with more salt and pepper if needed, and refrigerate until cold, at least 30 minutes and up to 1 day.

Heat 1 tablespoon of the olive oil in a large (12-inch) skillet over high heat until it's shimmering. Add the shrimp and cook, tossing, until it starts to brown and lose its raw color, about 2 minutes. Stir in the thyme, ½ teaspoon pepper, and ¼ teaspoon salt, and cook until the shrimp are just cooked through, about 1 minute. Transfer to a plate to cool.

Just before serving, cut the remainder of the cucumber into ¼-inch dice (about ½ cup) and toss with the remaining tablespoon extra-virgin olive oil, the remaining 1 teaspoon sherry vinegar, and ½ teaspoon salt. Serve the soup cold in individual bowls, garnished with the cucumber and shrimp.

MAKE IT LAST Unopened jarred or canned roasted red peppers will keep for months in the pantry; just check the sell-by date. Store jarred peppers in their jar. If canned, transfer them to an airtight plastic container after opening, and try to use them within a week or two. If you want to freeze the peppers, purée them in a food processor with a splash of olive oil and store in airtight container or zip-top bag in the freezer for two to three months.

The rich flavor and crunch of pine nuts are irresistible. Use them in everything from pesto to savory sides to sweets.

PINE NUTS

SAUTÉED SPINACH WITH GOLDEN RAISINS, PINE NUTS & FRESH BREADCRUMBS

This spinach side mixes the sweetness of raisins with savory garlic breadcrumbs. Making fresh breadcrumbs is simple. Use stale bread or toast fresh bread in a 300°F oven for a few minutes until crisp, and then pulse in a food processor until the bread is the size of peas.

Serves 4

¼ cup golden raisins
¼ cup pine nuts, toasted (see Toasting Nuts, below)
¼ cup olive oil
½ cup fresh, coarse breadcrumbs
1 large clove garlic, minced
Kosher salt
1 bunch (about 1 pound) spinach, trimmed

In a large (12-inch) skillet over medium heat, heat the raisins and pine nuts in 2 tablespoons oil for about 1 minute. With a slotted spoon, transfer the raisins and pine nuts to a plate. Add the breadcrumbs and garlic to the pan, and sprinkle with ¼ teaspoon salt. Cook over medium-low heat until slightly brown, 5 to 7 minutes. Transfer to a plate. Put the remaining 2 tablespoons oil in the pan with the spinach, and cook until the spinach just wilts. Transfer to a serving platter, toss with the raisins and pine nuts, top with breadcrumbs, and serve.

TOASTING NUTS

To toast pine nuts, you have two options. You can heat them in a skillet over medium-low heat on the stovetop until golden brown (tossing the nuts every 30 seconds or so to avoid scorching), about 5 to 10 minutes. Or toast them on a baking sheet in a 350°F oven (with a rack positioned in the center of the oven) until golden brown, about 7 to 10 minutes. The oven offers more even and gentle heat, though on the stovetop it's easier to watch the progress.

prep this

MINT & PINE NUT PESTO WITH GEMELLI & ASPARAGUS

Spread this pesto on top of chicken breasts or a firm-fleshed fish (anything from cod to salmon would work) and roast, or use as a spread on sandwiches or crostini. The combination of mint, scallions, and asparagus makes this dish perfect for spring.

Serves 4 to 6

FOR THE PESTO

6 scallions (dark and light green parts only), trimmed and thinly sliced (about ½ cup)

½ cup freshly grated Parmigiano-Reggiano

½ cup pine nuts, toasted (see Toasting Nuts, p. 41)

⅓ cup firmly packed fresh mint, chopped

5 tablespoons extra-virgin olive oil, more as needed

Kosher salt and freshly ground black pepper

FOR THE PASTA

1 pound gemelli

¾ pound asparagus, ends snapped off, cut into 1½-inch pieces

2 teaspoons fresh lemon juice, more to taste

¼ cup freshly grated Parmigiano-Reggiano

MAKE THE PESTO

Put the scallions, Parmigiano, pine nuts, and mint in a food processor and process until finely chopped. With the processor on, pour the oil down the feed tube in a steady stream, so the mixture thins into a slightly loose paste. Add more oil if needed. Add ½ teaspoon salt and ¾ teaspoon pepper and pulse once more. The pesto will keep in an airtight container in the refrigerator for up to four days.

MAKE THE PASTA

Bring a large (6-quart) pot of well-salted water to a boil over high heat. Add the pasta and cook, stirring occasionally, until nearly tender, about 2 minutes less than the package timing. Add the asparagus and cook with the pasta until both are tender, about 2 minutes more. Drain well and toss with the pesto and lemon juice. Add more lemon juice, salt, and pepper to taste. Serve sprinkled with black pepper and the Parmigiano.

ROSEMARY & PINE NUT COOKIES

These buttery crisps are like shortbread cookies with Italian flair. The fresh rosemary adds a wonderful fragrance and flavor while the toasted pine nuts both enrich the cookie dough and serve as a pretty decoration on top.

Serves 8

6¾ ounces (1½ cups) unbleached
   all-purpose flour

½ teaspoon baking soda

¼ teaspoon table salt

¾ cup granulated sugar

1½ teaspoons chopped fresh rosemary

6 ounces (¾ cup) unsalted butter,
   softened

1 large egg

½ teaspoon pure vanilla extract

½ cup pine nuts, toasted
   (see Toasting Nuts, p. 41)

In a medium bowl, combine the flour, baking soda, and salt until well blended, and set aside.

In a food processor, pulse the sugar and rosemary until combined and the rosemary is finely chopped. Transfer to a stand mixer fitted with the paddle attachment. Put all but 2 tablespoons of the pine nuts in the food processor and process until finely chopped.

Add the butter to the sugar mixture and beat on medium speed until light and fluffy, about 2 minutes. Reduce the speed to low and add the egg and vanilla; beat until thoroughly combined.

Add the chopped pine nuts and then the flour mixture and mix until the dough absorbs the flour and starts to come together.

Turn the dough out onto a large piece of plastic wrap and form into a log about 2 inches thick and 11 inches long. Wrap and refrigerate until firm, 1 to 2 hours.

Position a rack in the center of the oven and heat the oven to 350°F. Cut the dough into disks between ¼ and ½ inch thick (about 30 cookies). Sprinkle the cookies with the whole pine nuts and gently press in place so they adhere. Arrange on three baking sheets, spaced about 1½ inches apart. Bake one sheet at a time until the cookies are set and the sides are lightly brown, 10 to 12 minutes. Let cool for 10 minutes. Using a spatula, transfer the

cookies to a cooling rack and cool to room temperature, about 1 hour. Serve, or store in an airtight container at room temperature for up to five days.

MAKE IT LAST Like oils, seeds, and other nuts, pine nuts can go rancid. To avoid this, your best bet is to store them in a zip-top bag in the freezer, where they'll keep for up to six months.

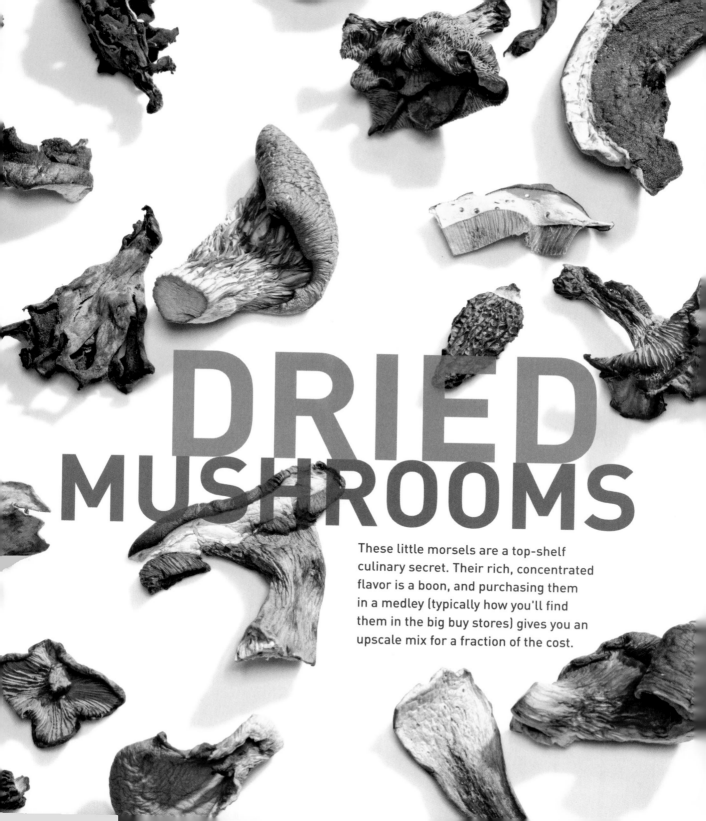

DRIED MUSHROOMS

These little morsels are a top-shelf culinary secret. Their rich, concentrated flavor is a boon, and purchasing them in a medley (typically how you'll find them in the big buy stores) gives you an upscale mix for a fraction of the cost.

CREAMY FONTINA POLENTA WITH
MUSHROOM RAGÙ

This warm and comforting side goes nicely with a hearty braise or beef stew.
Try coarse cornmeal instead of instant polenta. It has a more satisfying texture.

Serves 6

Kosher salt

1 cup coarse yellow cornmeal

2 tablespoons olive oil

4 ounces fresh cremini mushrooms, trimmed and sliced

1 medium clove garlic, minced

1½ cups (1 ounce) mixed dried mushrooms, rehydrated (see below) and chopped, plus ¾ cup soaking liquid

2 teaspoons chopped fresh thyme

Freshly ground black pepper

1½ cups grated Fontina (about 6 ounces)

REHYDRATING DRIED MUSHROOMS

Bring 2 cups water to a boil in a 2-quart saucepan, add the mushrooms, and boil for 3 minutes; remove the pot from the heat, cover and let sit for 20 minutes, or until the mushrooms become tender. Using a slotted spoon, transfer the mushrooms to a plate. Strain the soaking liquid through a coffee filter or a paper towel and reserve; yields about 1 cup of mushroom liquid.

prep this

Bring 4½ cups water to a boil in a 3-quart saucepan. Whisk in 1½ teaspoons salt and then the cornmeal. Reduce the heat to medium low and cook, stirring occasionally, until the cornmeal is tender and absorbs all the liquid, about 30 minutes.

Meanwhile, make the mushroom ragù. Heat the oil in a medium (10-inch) skillet over medium-high heat. Add the fresh mushrooms and cook, stirring, until they soften, 3 to 4 minutes. Reduce the heat to medium, add the garlic, and cook, stirring, until fragrant, about 1 minute. Add the rehydrated mushrooms and their liquid, thyme, ¼ teaspoon salt, and ½ teaspoon pepper; cover with the lid partially ajar and cook, stirring occasionally, until the liquid is a saucy consistency and the mushrooms soften, 7 to 8 minutes.

Stir the Fontina into the polenta. Taste and season with salt as needed. Serve the polenta topped with the ragù.

SEARED PORK MEDALLIONS IN
MARSALA-MUSHROOM SAUCE

The traditional flavors of chicken Marsala are taken in a completely different direction in this recipe by subbing rounds of pork tenderloin for the chicken cutlets. You can serve the dish over egg noodles or with an herb risotto.

Serves 4

1½ pounds pork tenderloin (1 large or 2 small), trimmed of fat and cut on the diagonal into 1½-inch rounds (about 8)

Kosher salt and freshly ground black pepper

½ cup unbleached all-purpose flour

2 tablespoons olive oil

1 tablespoon unsalted butter

1 large shallot, finely diced (about ¼ cup)

1½ cups (1 ounce) dried mushrooms, rehydrated (see Rehydrating Dried Mushrooms, p. 47) and chopped, plus ¾ cup soaking liquid

⅓ cup dry Marsala wine

¼ cup heavy cream

2 tablespoons chopped fresh flat-leaf parsley

Sprinkle the pork with 1 teaspoon salt and ½ teaspoon black pepper. Put the flour in a small bowl, and then dredge the pork in the flour, shaking off any excess.

Heat 1 tablespoon oil and the butter in a large (12-inch) heavy-duty skillet over medium heat until the butter melts. Add the pork and cook, without touching, until it starts to brown nicely and easily releases from the pan, about 4 minutes. Flip and cook the other sides in the same manner until the pork is cooked through and then transfer to a large serving platter. Cover loosely with foil.

To make the sauce, add the remaining 1 tablespoon oil and shallot to the pan, sprinkle with ¼ teaspoon salt, and cook, stirring, until the shallot softens and becomes translucent, about 2 minutes. Add the mushrooms and cook, stirring, for 1 minute. Add the Marsala, raise the heat to high, and cook, scraping the bottom of the pan with a wooden spoon to loosen any browned bits, until the liquid has almost completely reduced, about 2 minutes. Stir in the mushroom soaking liquid and cook until it reduces by about half, about 4 minutes. Whisk in the cream and bring to a boil. Take the sauce off the heat and spoon it over the pork. Serve sprinkled with parsley.

WILD MUSHROOM
& ARUGULA RISOTTO

Bulk dried mushrooms typically include more exotic types like oyster, shiitake, and morel. This satisfying risotto makes a meal on its own when accompanied by a green salad.

Serves 4

1½ cups (1 ounce) dried mushrooms, rehydrated (see Rehydrating Dried Mushrooms, p. 47) and chopped, plus ¾ cup soaking liquid

5 cups lower-salt chicken broth

4 tablespoons unsalted butter

1 medium yellow onion, finely diced (about 1 cup)

Kosher salt

1½ cups Carnaroli or Arborio rice

½ cup dry sherry

3 ounces baby arugula (4 cups, loosely packed)

1 cup freshly grated Parmigiano-Reggiano or Grana Padano

⅓ cup sliced chives

Freshly ground black pepper

Heat the mushroom soaking liquid with the chicken broth in a 3-quart saucepan over medium heat. Meanwhile, in a large (4-quart) pot, melt 2 tablespoons butter over medium-high heat. Add the onion and sprinkle with ½ teaspoon salt. Cook the onion, stirring, until it softens and turns a light brown, about 3 minutes. Add the rice and mushrooms and cook, stirring, for 1 minute. Add the sherry; raise the heat to high, and cook, stirring, until it almost completely reduces, about 1 minute.

Reduce the heat to medium; add ¾ cup of the broth to the rice, and cook, stirring often, until the rice absorbs the broth, 2 to 3 minutes. Add another ¾ cup of broth and cook until absorbed. Continue adding broth in this manner until the rice is creamy and tender, about 20 minutes total—you may or may not need all of the broth. Stir in the arugula, Parmigiano, all but a couple tablespoons of the chives, and the remaining 2 tablespoons butter and continue stirring until the arugula is just wilted, about 1 minute. Serve immediately in individual bowls, sprinkled with a few grinds of black pepper and the remaining chives.

MAKE IT LAST Dried mushrooms keep well in a zip-top bag or airtight container in a dry, cool place in your pantry for at least one year. If the mushrooms look discolored or grayish, they are probably beyond their shelf life and you should discard them.

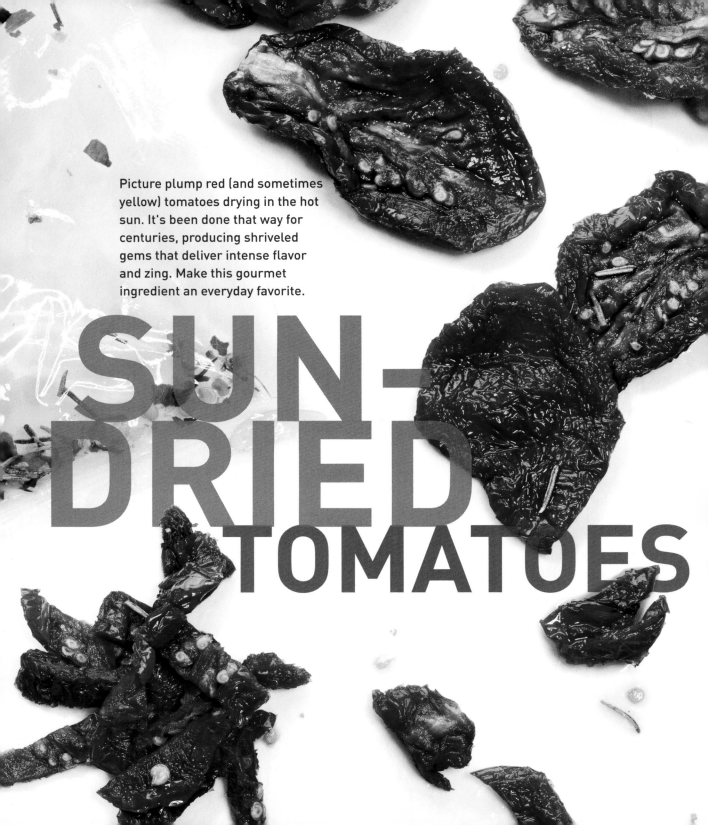

Picture plump red (and sometimes yellow) tomatoes drying in the hot sun. It's been done that way for centuries, producing shriveled gems that deliver intense flavor and zing. Make this gourmet ingredient an everyday favorite.

SUN-DRIED TOMATOES

SUN-DRIED TOMATO
& FETA VINAIGRETTE

Not only is this tangy dressing great on salads, but it's also delicious on boiled peeled baby potatoes. Using a bit of the oil from the sun-dried tomato jar infuses the dressing with added flavor. The dressing keeps for up to one week in the refrigerator.

Makes about 1½ cups

⅓ cup drained oil-packed sun-dried tomatoes, coarsely chopped, plus ¼ cup oil from the jar

¼ cup plus 2 tablespoons sherry vinegar

1 small shallot, coarsely chopped (about 3 tablespoons)

1 tablespoon loosely packed chopped fresh oregano

¼ teaspoon sweet pimentón (smoked paprika)

Kosher salt and freshly ground black pepper

½ cup extra-virgin olive oil

¼ cup crumbled feta cheese

Put the tomatoes, vinegar, shallot, oregano, pimentón, 1 teaspoon salt, ¼ teaspoon pepper, and 2 tablespoons water in a blender and blend to combine (don't worry if it doesn't purée; it will when you add the oil). With the blender running, pour the olive oil and the tomato oil in a slow, steady stream through the feed hole in the blender's lid. Transfer to a bowl or jar and stir in the feta. Season to taste with salt and pepper.

CHICKEN BREASTS STUFFED WITH SUN-DRIED TOMATOES & GREEN OLIVES

In this dish, sun-dried tomatoes are paired with mild, slightly smoky green olives, saffron, and honey for a savory chicken stuffing. But their intense flavor works well in just about any dish that calls for tomatoes—in pasta sauces and pesto, on pizza and bruschetta, and in tapenades and salads.

Serves 4

Pinch saffron (about 15 threads)
¼ cup extra-virgin olive oil
2½ teaspoons fresh lemon juice
1½ teaspoons mild honey, such as clover
½ teaspoon freshly grated lemon zest
¼ teaspoon crushed red pepper flakes
1 large clove garlic, crushed
Kosher salt
¼ cup drained oil-packed sun-dried
 tomatoes, very coarsely chopped
¼ cup pitted green olives, such as
 manzanilla
¼ cup loosely packed fresh flat-leaf
 parsley leaves, coarsely chopped
4 split skin-on bone-in chicken breasts
 (3 to 3½ pounds)
Freshly ground black pepper

Position a rack in the middle of the oven and heat the oven to 425°F.

Soak the saffron in 2 teaspoons hot water for 5 minutes. In a food processor, purée the saffron and soaking water with the olive oil, lemon juice, honey, lemon zest, red pepper flakes, garlic, and ½ teaspoon salt. Add the sun-dried tomatoes, olives, and parsley. Pulse to form a coarsely chopped stuffing (it should be coarser than pesto).

If any of the backbone is still attached to the chicken, cut it off with poultry shears. Trim off the side flap with rib meat and bones. Use your finger to make a small opening between the skin and the flesh of the breasts. Run your finger under the skin to separate it from the breasts, making a pocket and being careful not to detach the edges of the skin. Stuff the tomato mixture into the pocket, distributing it evenly over the chicken. Pat the skin back in place and season with 1 teaspoon salt and ½ teaspoon pepper. Line a heavy-duty rimmed baking sheet with aluminum foil. Roast the chicken on the baking sheet until the juices run clear and a meat thermometer registers 165°F, about 30 minutes.

MAKE IT LAST Sun-dried tomatoes keep for about a year. Upon opening, refrigerate oil-packed sun-dried tomatoes. They will keep for up to one month. Store dried sun-dried tomatoes (those not packed in oil) in a zip-top bag in the refrigerator for up to one year.

RIGATONI WITH SUN-DRIED TOMATO & FENNEL SAUCE

The sauce in this pasta dish is enhanced by the subtle licorice flavor of Pernod, but any pastis or anise-flavored liqueur could work. Add sliced, cooked sweet Italian sausage for a more substantial meal (its flavors work well with the sauce).

Serves 4

Kosher salt

2 tablespoons extra-virgin olive oil

1 cup chopped fennel (about ½ medium bulb)

2 medium cloves garlic, very coarsely chopped

1 cup heavy cream

1 cup lower-salt chicken broth

⅓ cup drained oil-packed sun-dried tomatoes, very coarsely chopped

¼ teaspoon crushed red pepper flakes

1 tablespoon Pernod (optional)

1 pound rigatoni

Bring a large pot of well-salted water to a boil. Meanwhile, heat the olive oil in a 10- to 11-inch straight-sided sauté pan over medium heat. Add the fennel and garlic and cook, stirring occasionally, until the fennel starts to soften and brown, about 5 minutes. Stir in 1 cup water, the cream, chicken broth, sun-dried tomatoes, red pepper flakes, and 1 teaspoon salt. Bring to a boil, reduce the heat, and simmer briskly, uncovered, until the tomatoes are plump and soft, about 15 minutes.

Remove from the heat and stir in the Pernod®, if using. Let cool slightly and then purée in a blender until smooth. Wipe out the skillet, return the sauce to the skillet, season to taste with salt, and keep hot.

Cook the rigatoni until just barely al dente, 1 to 2 minutes less than the package instructions. Drain well and return to the pot. Add the sauce and toss over medium-low heat for a minute or two so the pasta finishes cooking and absorbs some of the sauce.

DAIRY

Grana Padano is a perfect choice when you are craving the rich, sharp flavor of hard Italian cheese. It is a milder alternative to Parmigiano-Reggiano and sure to satisfy any palate.

GRANA PADANO

SPINACH, CHEESE & CARAMELIZED RED ONION FRITTATA

This Italian omelet is perfect for brunch or a quick weeknight dinner. It also reheats nicely in the microwave as a midday snack. To add heft, fold diced boiled potatoes into the spinach mixture before adding it to the eggs. Incorporating strips of roasted red peppers adds more color.

Serves 8

¼ cup olive oil

1 large red onion, thinly sliced (about 1 cup)

Kosher salt

1 jalapeño, cored, seeded, and finely diced (about 2 tablespoons)

10 ounces whole leaf spinach, trimmed, washed, and spun dry

10 large eggs, beaten

1¼ cups freshly grated Grana Padano

3 oil-packed sun-dried tomatoes, finely diced (about 2 tablespoons)

8 basil leaves, torn into small pieces

Freshly ground black pepper

Position a rack in the center of the oven and heat the oven to 450°F.

Heat 2 tablespoons oil in a large (12-inch), ovenproof, nonstick skillet over medium-high heat. Add the onion, sprinkle with ½ teaspoon salt, and cook, stirring until it starts to color and soften, about 2 minutes. Reduce the heat to medium, add the jalapeño, and continue cooking until the onion softens almost completely, about 5 minutes. Add the spinach, sprinkle with ½ teaspoon salt, increase the heat to high, and cook, tossing, until the spinach just wilts, about 2 minutes. Remove from the heat and let cool for a couple of minutes.

In a large bowl, whisk the eggs with the Grana Padano, sun-dried tomatoes, basil, 1 teaspoon pepper, and ¼ teaspoon salt. Add the vegetables from the skillet to the egg mixture and stir to combine.

Wipe the skillet with a paper towel and heat the remaining 2 tablespoons oil in it over medium heat. Add the egg mixture and cook, running a spatula along the bottom of the pan to prevent sticking, until the eggs begin to set around the edges, about 3 minutes. Transfer the skillet to the oven and bake until the eggs puff and are firm to the touch and browned on top, about 12 minutes. Let cool for a couple minutes, then slide onto a cutting board, cut into wedges, and serve.

ORECCHIETTE WITH HAM & PEAS IN CHEESE SAUCE

In this dressed-up macaroni and cheese, orecchiette takes the place of tiny elbows, peas and ham add flavor and texture, and Grana Padano stands in for the usual Cheddar.

Serves 8

Kosher salt

1 pound orecchiette or other small shell pasta

1/2 cup unsalted butter, more for the dish

1 large shallot, finely diced (about 1/4 cup)

1/4 cup unbleached all-purpose flour

3 cups whole milk, warmed

2 cups freshly grated Grana Padano

2 teaspoons chopped fresh thyme

Freshly ground black pepper

1/4 teaspoon Tabasco

3/4 pound ham steak, cut into 1/2-inch dice

2 cups frozen peas, thawed

1/2 cup coarse fresh breadcrumbs

1 tablespoon olive oil

Position a rack in the center of the oven and heat the oven to 375°F. Butter a 9x13-inch baking dish.

Bring a large pot of well-salted water to a boil and add the pasta; cook according to package directions until al dente. Reserve 1/2 cup of the pasta water, drain the pasta well, and return the pasta to the pot.

Meanwhile, for the cheese sauce, melt the butter in a medium (3-quart) saucepan over medium heat. Add the shallot, sprinkle with 1/4 teaspoon salt, and cook, stirring occasionally, until it softens and becomes translucent, about 3 minutes. Add the flour and cook, stirring, until it turns golden and smells nutty, about 1 minute. Whisk in the milk in a slow, steady stream, and cook, whisking occasionally to avoid sticking on the bottom of the pan, until the mixture thickens, about 10 minutes. Remove from the heat and stir in all but 1/2 cup of Grana Padano, the thyme, 1 1/2 teaspoons black pepper, 1/2 teaspoon salt, and the Tabasco. Stir the ham and peas into the béchamel; taste and add more salt and pepper if needed.

Stir 1/4 cup of the pasta water into the béchamel so it loosens a bit and then toss with the pasta in the pasta pot. Add more pasta water as needed. Transfer to the prepared baking dish. In a small bowl, mix the breadcrumbs, olive oil, 1/4 teaspoon salt, and 1/4 teaspoon pepper with the remaining 1/2 cup cheese, and sprinkle over the pasta. Bake the pasta until it bubbles and browns around the edges, about 20 minutes (cover with foil if the top browns too quickly). Let cool for a couple of minutes and then serve.

BAKED EGGPLANT
"PARMESAN"

For the marinara, you can use your own sauce or try the Quick Marinara with Toasted Garlic & Rosemary (p. 23). Serve this hearty dish with a portion of pasta or between two slices of toasted Italian bread for a delicious sandwich.

Serves 6 to 8

2 medium globe eggplant (about 2 pounds),
    cut crosswise into ¼-inch-thick rounds
Kosher salt
4½ ounces (1 cup) unbleached
    all-purpose flour
4 large eggs, beaten
3 cups dry fine breadcrumbs
2 teaspoons chopped fresh thyme
Canola oil for frying (about 2 cups)
3 cups marinara sauce, warmed
16 basil leaves, torn into large pieces
10 ounces fresh mozzarella,
    thinly sliced (about 2 cups)
1½ cups freshly grated Grana Padano

Line a large plate with paper towels. Put down a layer of eggplant slices, sprinkle generously with salt; add another layer of paper towels and another layer of eggplant and salt; repeat until you've layered the rest of the eggplant. Let sit for 20 minutes.

Put the flour and eggs in separate wide shallow bowls. In another wide bowl, toss the breadcrumbs with the thyme and ½ teaspoon salt. Line a baking sheet with paper towels. Dredge the eggplant slices in the flour, dip in the egg, and then coat with the breadcrumbs, pressing down to pat the crumbs onto the eggplant, and put on the baking sheet.

Line another baking sheet with fresh paper towels. Pour enough oil into a large (12-inch) skillet or frying pan to measure about ½ inch deep and heat over medium heat until hot (if you dip a piece of eggplant into the oil, it will sizzle immediately). Working in batches, add as much eggplant as will fit in a single layer and fry, flipping once, until golden brown, 1 to 2 minutes per side. Transfer to the baking sheet. Repeat, frying the remaining eggplant and layering it between sheets of paper towel.

continued

MAKE IT LAST To store Grana Padano, simply wrap it in a few layers of parchment, waxed paper, or foil and put it in the crisper drawer of the refrigerator. It will keep for about three weeks; if any mold develops on the surface of the cheese, shave off the moldy parts and surrounding area. The rest of the cheese is still good.

Position a rack in the center of the oven and heat the oven to 425°F. Arrange a layer of eggplant in a 9x13-inch baking dish. Top with 1 cup of the marinara and then cover with a third of the basil, mozzarella, and Grana Padano. Repeat with two more layers of the remaining eggplant, marinara, basil, mozzarella, and Grana Padano.

Bake until the cheese melts and browns and the sauce bubbles around the edges, 25 to 30 minutes (cover with foil if the top browns too quickly). Let cool for a couple minutes and serve.

WHAT IS GRANA PADANO?

Like Parmigiano-Reggiano, Grana Padano is a well-aged, semi-fat, hard cheese made from cow's milk. To be labeled as Grana Padano, like Parmigiano-Reggiano, the cheese must be made in certain areas of northern Italy, following strict quality guidelines, and aged for a considerable amount of time (up to 18 months). Grana Padano tends to have a milder flavor and less grainy texture than Parmigiano.

Traditionally a brined sheep's milk cheese, feta is crumbly, salty, and moist. It is a versatile ingredient that gives any dish an instant hit of flavor and is perfect in salads, pizzas, and wraps.

FETA

GRILLED LAMB BURGERS WITH MARINATED RED ONIONS, DILL & SLICED FETA

When you tire of the basic burger, this Mediterranean-inspired version is just the ticket. The quick-pickled red onions add dimension and are a great addition to cucumber, tomato, and pasta salads. To keep with the Greek theme, serve the burgers in warm pita bread, though whole-wheat hamburger buns would work, too.

Serves 4

1¼ pounds ground lamb

2 teaspoons sweet paprika

2 teaspoons dried oregano

1 small clove garlic, minced and mashed to a paste

Kosher salt

6 ounces feta, cut into ¼-inch-thick slices (about 8)

2 tablespoons extra-virgin olive oil

2 tablespoons chopped fresh dill

½ small red onion, thinly sliced

3 tablespoons red-wine vinegar

1 teaspoon granulated sugar

4 whole-wheat pita bread, warmed

4 thin slices tomato

8 thin slices English cucumber

Prepare a medium charcoal or gas grill fire. Clean and oil the grill grates. Gently mix the lamb with the paprika, oregano, garlic, and 1 teaspoon salt. Form into four ½-inch-thick patties.

On a large plate, lay out the slices of feta and sprinkle with the olive oil and 1 tablespoon of the dill. In a small bowl, toss the onion with the vinegar, sugar, ½ teaspoon salt, and the remaining 1 tablespoon dill, and let sit for 10 to 15 minutes at room temperature.

Grill the burgers on one side until they have good grill marks, about 5 minutes. Flip and cook the other side until it has good grill marks, too, and the burgers are just light pink inside (make a nick with a paring knife), about 5 minutes for medium doneness.

Serve the burgers in the warmed pita with the feta, tomato, cucumber, and a heaping teaspoon of pickled onions.

MAKE IT LAST Feta is best stored in the salty brine it is sometimes packed in. Once opened, it will keep in the refrigerator for at least a week. If the cheese is not in brine, mix 1 cup water with ¼ cup kosher salt to make a quick brine, and refrigerate in an airtight container.

BAKED ORZO WITH SHRIMP, LEMON & FETA

All sorts of ingredients—sun-dried tomatoes, olives, peas, or corn—can be added to this baked pasta for extra flavor and color. Serve this side with a seared steak for a Mediterranean version of surf and turf.

Serves 6 to 8

5 tablespoons olive oil, more for the dish

1 pound shrimp (26 to 30 per pound), peeled and deveined

Kosher salt and freshly ground black pepper

1 large clove garlic, minced

5 ounces baby spinach

1 pound orzo

6 ounces feta, crumbled (about 1½ cups)

2 teaspoons chopped fresh thyme

Finely grated zest of 1 lemon

¾ cup Panko

FETA PLAYS WELL WITH OTHERS

Feta's wonderful mix of tangy, salty, and creamy notes make it a versatile ingredient perfect in a number of dishes. Crumble it and use as a sharper version of queso fresco for topping tacos or tortilla soup. Pair it with black olives and grilled chicken for an easy, flavorful pizza topping. Or make a simple salad of feta, cherry tomatoes, and thinly sliced scallions.

Position a rack in the center of the oven and heat the oven to 425°F. Bring a large pot of well-salted water to a boil. Lightly coat a 2-quart baking dish with oil.

Heat 2 tablespoons oil in a 12-inch skillet over medium-high heat until shimmering. Add the shrimp, sprinkle with ½ teaspoon each salt and pepper, and cook, stirring, until the shrimp start to lose their raw color (but don't cook through), about 2 minutes. Add the garlic and cook, stirring, for 30 seconds. Stir in the spinach and cook, tossing, until it starts to wilt, about 1 minute. Remove from the heat.

Add the pasta to the boiling water and cook according to the package instructions until al dente. Drain well and toss with the shrimp mixture, feta, 2 tablespoons oil, half the thyme, and lemon zest. Transfer to the prepared baking dish. In a small bowl, toss the breadcrumbs with the remaining tablespoon oil, the remaining teaspoon thyme, and ¼ teaspoon salt. Sprinkle on top of the pasta.

Bake the pasta until the breadcrumbs brown and the pasta heats through, about 20 minutes (cover with foil if the top browns too quickly). Let cool for a couple of minutes and then serve.

WATERMELON, HEIRLOOM TOMATO & FETA SALAD

Watermelon might seem like an unexpected match for the tomatoes and cheese in this salad, but the fruit's sweetness complements the salty, creamy notes in the feta. For a pretty presentation, thinly slice the tomatoes, feta, and watermelon and arrange them in layers, or make the slices bite-size and skewer them for an appetizer.

Serves 6 to 8

2 large yellow tomatoes (about 1¼ pounds), cored and cut into ¾-inch pieces

1 pound seedless watermelon, trimmed of rind and cut into ¾-inch pieces

2 tablespoons chopped fresh mint

6 tablespoons extra-virgin olive oil

1½ tablespoons red-wine vinegar

Kosher salt

¼ teaspoon crushed red pepper flakes

8 ounces feta, cut into ¾-inch pieces

Coarse sea salt (optional)

Combine the tomatoes, watermelon, and mint in a large serving bowl. In a small bowl, whisk together the oil, vinegar, 1 teaspoon salt, and the red pepper flakes. Pour over the tomato mixture and toss well. Let the mixture sit for 15 minutes at room temperature. Fold in the feta and toss well.

Serve, sprinkled lightly with the coarse sea salt, if using (use about ½ teaspoon—it adds a bit of texture); this salad can sit for 1 to 2 hours at room temperature.

BRIE

The thrill of buying a wheel of brie is matched by how deliciously easy it is to use it up. It elevates the most basic cheese platter and is irresistible when spread on crusty breads or paired with just about any fruit.

CROSTINI WITH BRIE, DATES & TOASTED WALNUTS

This nibble builds on the classic pairing of cheese, dried fruit, and nuts. A splash of balsamic vinegar helps bring together all the flavors. The crostini are best served right out of the oven, though they can also hold for an hour or two at room temperature.

Serves 8

1 medium baguette (about ½ pound), sliced into ½-inch rounds (about 24 slices)

2 tablespoons olive oil

Kosher salt

½ cup coarsely chopped toasted walnuts (see Toasting Nuts, p. 41)

½ cup Medjool dates (about 6 to 8), pitted and coarsely chopped

1 tablespoon honey

1 tablespoon balsamic vinegar

6 ounces brie, rind trimmed and softened to room temperature

2 tablespoons thinly sliced chives

Position a rack in the center of the oven and heat the oven to 425°F. Set the bread slices on a large baking sheet; dab both sides with the oil and sprinkle one side lightly with salt (about ¼ teaspoon for all the bread). Bake until the bread starts to brown and crisp, about 8 minutes. Meanwhile, in a medium bowl, toss the walnuts with the dates, honey, and vinegar.

While the bread is still warm, spread with brie and then top with the date and nut mixture. Sprinkle with the chives and serve.

MAKE IT LAST A rule of thumb with cheese is that the softer it is, the quicker it will go bad. Brie is a soft cheese and has a shorter shelf life than hard cheeses like Pecorino-Romano. Unopened in its original packaging, brie will keep for at least one month in the refrigerator. Once opened and cut into wedges, wrap the cheese in plastic wrap, refrigerate, and try to use within a week.

OVEN-TOASTED HAM, BRIE & APPLE SANDWICHES

Remove the rind from the brie while the cheese is still cold, and choose a thinly sliced ham steak rather than deli ham for a meaty flavor and texture. Look for a ham steak that's labeled "ham in natural juices."

Serves 4

1 large baguette (about 1 pound), cut into 4 pieces

7 ounces brie, most of the rind trimmed off and thinly sliced

2 tablespoons unsalted butter

1½ medium Granny Smith apples, peeled (optional), cored, and cut into ¼-inch-thick wedges (about 1½ cups)

¾ pound ham steak, thinly sliced on the diagonal

2 tablespoons whole-grain Dijon mustard

1 tablespoon honey

1 teaspoon chopped fresh thyme

Position a rack in the center of the oven and heat the oven to 425°F. Split the baguette pieces lengthwise, open them up like a book, and top one side with the brie. Set on a baking sheet lined with parchment paper or aluminum foil, and bake until the cheese melts and the bread lightly browns, about 5 minutes.

Meanwhile, melt the butter in a large (12-inch) heavy-duty skillet over medium-high heat. Add the apples and cook, tossing every minute or so, until they start to soften and brown in places, 3 to 4 minutes. Add the ham and cook, gently tossing, until it warms. Remove from the heat and gently toss with the mustard, honey, and thyme until the ham and apples are evenly coated. Using tongs, distribute the ham mixture into the warm pieces of baguette, secure with 2 toothpicks, cut in half, and serve.

USING LEFTOVER BRIE
Though brie is traditionally used as a spread for crackers or bread, it's also a delicious ingredient in savory cooking. Try folding leftover brie into mashed potatoes, risotto, or polenta where it will add sharp richness—just be sure to remove the rind.

BRIE FONDUE
WITH FRESH THYME & CHARDONNAY

The fresh herbs and wine in this fondue add a decadency that masks how simple it is to prepare. Play up this entertaining classic by stirring in luxurious ingredients like fresh lobster, crabmeat, sautéed mushrooms, or spinach. Crisp tart apple slices are good for dipping; you can also use carrot sticks, roasted potato wedges, or bread cubes.

Serves 8

2 tablespoons unsalted butter

1 large shallot, finely diced (about ¼ cup)

½ cup Chardonnay

1 pound brie, rind removed and cut into
   1-inch pieces

1½ tablespoons cornstarch

2 teaspoons chopped fresh thyme

Freshly ground black pepper

Kosher salt

4 medium Fuji apples (or Macoun), cored
   and cut into 1-inch slices (about 4 cups)

Melt the butter in a medium (3-quart) saucepan over medium heat. Add the shallot and cook, stirring occasionally, until soft and translucent, about 3 minutes. Add the Chardonnay and ¼ cup water, and bring to a simmer. In a small bowl, toss the brie with the cornstarch to coat and then whisk into the wine until the cheese completely melts, about 2 minutes. Stir in the thyme and ½ teaspoon black pepper. Taste and add more pepper or salt if needed. Transfer to a fondue pot, set out long skewers, and let guests serve themselves by dipping the apple slices into the fondue.

TO RIND OR NOT TO RIND
The rind of this cheese is most definitely edible but whether or not you eat it is a matter of personal taste. It has an intense flavor that is pleasing to some palates and overpowering to others. In the brie recipes in this book, the rind was removed to create a uniform texture and flavor. When baking the cheese or serving it at room temperature, leave the rind on, as it holds the cheese together.

PLAIN YOGURT

Plain yogurt can take on almost any flavor. It is great on its own and works well in sweet and savory dishes alike. It's also one of only a few ingredients that tenderizes as it marinates.

YOGURT CAKE
WITH CHOCOLATE GANACHE FROSTING

Yogurt adds moisture to this dense cake's crumb and a light tartness that breaks up the richness of the ganache frosting. Dairy tends to dull the flavor of cocoa, so we decided on a vanilla cake instead of a chocolate one, but chocolate lovers can still get their fix from the cake's heavenly chocolate ganache icing.

Serves 12

FOR THE CAKE
4 ounces (½ cup) unsalted butter, softened, more for the pan
9 ounces (2 cups) unbleached all-purpose flour
1 teaspoon baking powder
1 teaspoon baking soda
¼ teaspoon table salt
1 cup granulated sugar
3 large eggs
1½ cups plain yogurt (low-fat or full-fat)
2 teaspoons pure vanilla extract

FOR THE GANACHE FROSTING
¾ cup heavy cream
8 ounces semisweet chocolate, broken into small pieces
1 tablespoon light corn syrup

MAKE THE CAKE
Position a rack in the center of the oven and heat the oven to 350°F. Butter a 9-inch cake pan. Line the pan with a piece of parchment paper cut to size.

In a medium bowl, whisk together the flour, baking powder, baking soda, and salt. In a stand mixer fitted with a paddle attachment or in a large bowl with an electric hand mixer, cream the sugar and butter on medium speed until smooth and fluffy. Reduce the speed to low, add the eggs, and then add the yogurt and vanilla, scraping down the sides of the bowl as needed. Add the dry ingredients and mix until just incorporated.

Transfer the batter to the prepared pan and bake until a toothpick inserted into the center comes out clean, about 45 minutes. Let cool completely on a rack before turning the cake out of the pan.

MAKE THE FROSTING
Bring the cream to a simmer in a small saucepan over medium heat. Reduce the heat to low, add the chocolate and corn syrup, and whisk until the chocolate is completely melted. Remove from the heat and let cool for 15 minutes. Transfer to a large bowl and refrigerate uncovered, stirring every 30 minutes or so, until it firms to a spreadable texture, about 45 minutes.

continued

TO SERVE

Transfer the cake to a cake plate. Frost the cake and
serve right away, or refrigerate for up to five days in an
airtight cake container (return to room temperature
before serving).

BAKING AND COOKING (AND MORE) WITH YOGURT

In many recipes, yogurt is a lower-fat substitution for richer ingredients like butter
or oil. And like buttermilk or sour cream, yogurt not only adds tang to cakes but it also
helps to create a moist texture. Beyond that, yogurt is a great base for fruit smoothies
and parfaits mixed with fresh fruit and granola.

left: **yogurt cake** with chocolate ganache frosting

GRILLED CHICKEN
TANDOORI

Plain yogurt is the base for the chicken marinade and keeps the meat moist and tender. Marinate the chicken for a day or two in the fridge for the most flavorful results. Chipotle powder, not typically used in Tandoori recipes, adds a welcome touch of heat and smokiness. For a well-rounded meal, serve the chicken with grilled peppers and onions and steamed basmati rice.

Serves 4

4 pounds skinless chicken parts, rinsed and patted dry

1 cup plain yogurt

2 tablespoons tomato paste

2 tablespoons minced fresh ginger

2 medium cloves garlic, minced (about 1½ teaspoons)

1½ tablespoons curry powder

1 teaspoon chipotle powder

Kosher salt and freshly ground black pepper

2 tablespoons chopped fresh cilantro

1 lime, cut into wedges

Put the chicken in a large bowl. In a small bowl, mix the yogurt with the tomato paste, ginger, garlic, curry powder, chipotle powder, 1½ teaspoons salt, and ¾ teaspoon pepper. Toss with the chicken. Cover and refrigerate for up to two days, or let sit at room temperature while the grill heats.

Prepare a medium charcoal or gas grill fire. Clean and oil the grill grates. Grill the chicken, covered, until it has good grill marks, about 5 minutes. Turn and continue cooking until the chicken is browned all over and cooked through (make a nick in a couple of the thicker pieces with a paring knife), about 15 to 20 minutes total. Set on a platter, sprinkle with the cilantro, and serve with the lime wedges for squeezing.

MAKE IT LAST There is no trick to storing yogurt beyond properly refrigerating it and keeping an eye on its sell-by date. Typically, yogurt does not freeze well—it loses its creamy texture when thawed.

VEGETABLE CRUDITÉS WITH JALAPEÑO DIPPING SAUCE

The heat of a jalapeño spices up this refreshing vegetable dip. A tangy alternative with less heat would be to substitute a teaspoon of lime juice for the jalapeño. Dig in with any of your favorite vegetables, like carrots, asparagus, red pepper slices, cherry tomatoes, broccoli, celery, or fennel.

Serves 8 to 10

2 cups plain yogurt
   (preferably not fat-free)
⅓ cup jarred jalapeño slices,
   drained well
1 small clove garlic, minced and
   mashed to a paste
Kosher salt and freshly ground
   black pepper
¼ cup chopped fresh cilantro
2 teaspoons chopped fresh thyme
3 pounds fresh vegetables, trimmed,
   for dipping

In a food processor, pulse the yogurt, jalapeños, garlic, ½ teaspoon salt, and ½ teaspoon pepper until uniform but slightly chunky, about 1 to 2 pulses. Transfer to a medium bowl and stir in the cilantro and thyme. Taste and season with more salt and pepper if needed. (You can refrigerate for up to one day before serving.) Serve with the vegetables.

CHEDDAR

Whether in your favorite comfort food or showcased in more adventurous preparations, Cheddar is a kitchen mainstay. Scrumptious at breakfast, lunch, and dinner, its zing and bite are always crowd-pleasers.

POBLANOS STUFFED WITH CHEDDAR & CHICKEN

Traditional chile rellenos are stuffed, coated in an egg batter, and fried. This stuffed pepper variation has no breading, making a lighter meal. Removing the seeds and white inner membrane of the pepper ensures they won't be too hot; substitute black beans for the chicken to create a vegetarian variation of the dish.

Serves 4

4 large poblano chiles

2 medium tomatoes, chopped

½ medium white onion, chopped

1 large clove garlic, chopped

1 teaspoon dried oregano, crumbled

1 teaspoon ground cumin

Generous pinch ground cinnamon

Kosher salt

1 tablespoon olive oil

2 cups shredded cooked chicken, preferably dark meat

1½ cups cooked brown or white rice

2 cups grated sharp or extra-sharp white Cheddar (about 7 ounces)

¼ cup chopped fresh cilantro (including some tender stems)

1 tablespoon fresh lime juice

Position an oven rack about 4 inches from the broiler and heat the broiler on high. Line a large rimmed baking sheet with foil.

Slit the chiles from stem to tip and set on the baking sheet. Broil, turning every few minutes, until blackened all over, 5 to 8 minutes. Let cool slightly, peel off the skins, and cut out the seed cores, leaving the stems on. Turn the chiles inside out, flick out any remaining seeds, and turn right side out. Return the poblanos to the baking sheet.

Purée the tomatoes, onion, garlic, oregano, cumin, cinnamon, and ½ teaspoon salt in a food processor. Heat the oil in a 12-inch skillet over medium heat. Add the purée and cook, stirring frequently, until the liquid has evaporated and the mixture looks thick and pulpy, 8 to 11 minutes. Remove the pan from the heat. Stir in the chicken and rice, and then 1 cup of the cheese, the cilantro, and the lime juice. Season to taste with salt. Divide the filling among the peppers, wrapping the sides of the peppers up and around the filling, some of which will still be exposed.

Broil the peppers until the cheese is melting and the tops begin to brown, about 4 minutes. Top with the remaining 1 cup cheese and broil until the cheese is completely melted, about 2 minutes.

CHEDDAR
& CAULIFLOWER SOUP

Depending on how much you enjoy the intense flavor of Cheddar, choose between a sharp or extra-sharp version of the cheese for this rustic soup. To dress it up for a special occasion, garnish with a combination of 3 tablespoons of chopped toasted walnuts, 1 tablespoon of chopped fresh flat-leaf parsley, and 1½ teaspoons of finely grated lemon zest.

Makes 8 cups; serves 6 to 8

Kosher salt

½ head cauliflower (about 1 pound), cored and cut into 1½-inch florets

2 tablespoons unsalted butter

1 medium yellow onion, finely diced

1 medium clove garlic, minced

2 tablespoons unbleached all-purpose flour

¼ teaspoon packed freshly grated nutmeg

⅛ teaspoon cayenne

2 cups lower-salt chicken broth

½ cup heavy cream

3 sprigs fresh thyme

4 cups grated sharp or extra-sharp white Cheddar (about 14 ounces)

Freshly ground black pepper

Bring a large pot of salted water to a boil. Boil the cauliflower until tender, about 4 minutes. Drain and let cool slightly. Trim the stems from 18 of the cauliflower pieces and cut the crowns into mini florets about ½ inch wide; set aside. Reserve the trimmed stems with the remaining larger pieces.

Melt the butter in a 4-quart saucepan over medium-low heat. Add the onion and ¼ teaspoon salt and cook, stirring frequently, until soft, 10 to 12 minutes.

Add the garlic and cook until the aroma subsides, 2 to 3 minutes. Increase the heat to medium, add the flour, nutmeg, and cayenne and cook for 3 minutes, stirring constantly. Whisk in the broth, cream, and 2 cups water. Add the thyme and bring to a simmer. Stir in the cheese until melted and simmer for 5 minutes to develop the flavors.

Remove and discard the thyme stems and stir in the larger cauliflower pieces and reserved stems. Working in batches, purée the soup in a blender. Return the soup to the pot, and season with salt and black pepper to taste. Add the mini cauliflower florets and reheat gently before serving.

BREAKING DOWN CHEDDAR

The longer Cheddar is aged, the more pronounced and sharp its flavor becomes. In turn, it also develops a grainier (or less creamy) texture. Some prefer young, mild Cheddar for grating and melting, but for that unmistakable bite, go with sharp or aged Cheddar.

BAKED CHEDDAR GRITS WITH BACON

Bacon and Cheddar give simple grits a new lease on life. Whipped egg whites lighten the grits, making for a soufflé-like texture.

Serves 6

Kosher salt

1 cup hominy grits (not instant or quick), such as Quaker® Old Fashioned Grits

1½ cups grated sharp or extra-sharp white Cheddar (about 5 ounces)

1 tablespoon unbleached all-purpose flour

1 teaspoon chopped fresh thyme

Freshly ground black pepper

1 medium clove garlic

6 strips bacon (about 6 ounces), cooked until crisp and chopped into small bits

3 large eggs, separated

¼ cup heavy cream

Position a rack in the center of the oven and heat the oven to 350°F.

Put 4½ cups water and ½ teaspoon salt in a 4-quart saucepan, cover, and bring to a boil. Whisk the grits into the pan in a slow stream. Reduce the heat to medium low, cover, and simmer, whisking occasionally, until thickened, 12 to 15 minutes.

In a large bowl, toss 1¼ cups of the cheese, the flour, thyme, and several grinds of pepper. Chop the garlic, sprinkle with a generous pinch of salt, and mash it into a paste with the side of a chef's knife. Whisk the mashed garlic, the cheese mixture, and the bacon into the grits until blended and the cheese is melted. Season to taste with salt and pepper.

Scrape the grits into the large bowl. In a medium bowl, beat the egg whites and a pinch of salt with a hand mixer until they just hold stiff peaks. In a small bowl, whisk the yolks and cream; whisk this mixture into the grits. With a large spatula, gently stir one-third of the whites into the grits to lighten them and then fold in the remaining whites. Scrape the grits into an 8x8x2-inch glass or ceramic baking dish.

Sprinkle the remaining ¼ cup cheese evenly over the grits. Bake until puffed, browned, and bubbling, 50 minutes to 1 hour.

MAKE IT LAST Check the cheese's sell-by date before purchase—be sure it's at least a month away. Once you've gotten the Cheddar home and have removed its original packaging, store it in the refrigerator by wrapping it first in parchment or waxed paper and then in a layer of plastic wrap or foil. It will keep for several weeks. If any mold develops, simply cut it away, about ½ inch below the mold. If the cheese emits any off-odors or becomes slimy, discard it.

MEAT & FISH

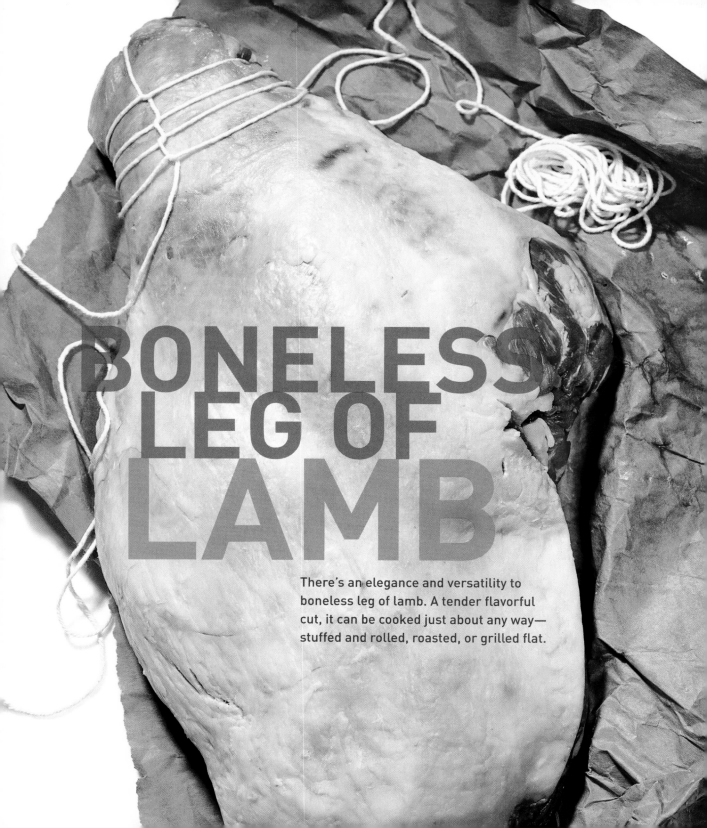

BONELESS LEG OF LAMB

There's an elegance and versatility to boneless leg of lamb. A tender flavorful cut, it can be cooked just about any way—stuffed and rolled, roasted, or grilled flat.

ROAST LEG OF LAMB
STUFFED WITH BASIL PESTO

The soy sauce in the marinade may sound like an unusual pairing with the pesto, but it intensifies the flavor of the meat without unduly standing out. Searing the meat first gives it a caramelized crust and roasting the lamb means easy, hands-off meal preparation.

Serves 4 to 6

5 pounds boneless leg of lamb, trimmed of fat

¼ cup reduced-sodium soy sauce

7 tablespoons olive oil

2 teaspoons chopped fresh thyme

2 cloves garlic, finely chopped (about 2 teaspoons)

Kosher salt and freshly ground black pepper

1 packed cup basil leaves

⅓ cup walnuts, toasted and coarsely chopped (see Toasting Nuts, p. 41)

⅓ cup freshly grated Parmigiano-Reggiano

¼ cup plain dry breadcrumbs

SEASON THE LAMB

Because lamb has a strong, assertive flavor, try to season or marinate it for a couple hours or a day ahead so that the seasonings have a chance to take hold. Strong acidic ingredients like lemon or red wine cut through the meat's gamey flavor, while garlic and chopped fresh herbs form an aromatic base.

prep this

Set the lamb in the middle of a large cutting board. Make deep horizontal slices into the thicker parts of the meat so you can open the lamb up like a book and even out the meat's overall thickness to about ½ inch; discard any additional fatty patches. Using a meat mallet or the bottom of a heavy skillet, gently pound the lamb to flatten it slightly and make its thickness even more uniform.

Put the lamb into a large non-reactive dish. In a small bowl, mix the soy sauce, 2 tablespoons oil, the thyme, and garlic with 1 teaspoon salt and ½ teaspoon pepper. Sprinkle all over the lamb, cover, and refrigerate for at least 4 hours and up to 2 days.

In a food processor, combine the basil, walnuts, Parmigiano-Reggiano, 3 tablespoons oil, and ¼ teaspoon each salt and pepper; process until the mixture turns into a paste. Transfer to a medium bowl. Sprinkle the lamb with ½ teaspoon salt, turn it over, and evenly distribute the pesto and breadcrumbs. Roll up the lamb (pesto side in), secure in 5 or 6 places with kitchen twine, and sprinkle with ½ teaspoon each salt and pepper.

Position a rack in the center of the oven and heat the oven to 325°F. Heat the remaining oil in a 12-inch (or larger) skillet over medium-high heat. Set the lamb in the skillet and brown the meat on all sides, about 2 minutes per side for a total of 8 minutes.

Transfer the lamb to a roasting pan and roast in the oven until an instant-read thermometer inserted into the

thickest part of the meat registers 135°F for medium-rare, about 40 to 45 minutes. Transfer the lamb to a cutting board, tent with foil, and let rest for 10 minutes. Thinly slice and serve.

LEG OF LAMB
WITH TARRAGON & FRESH MINT SAUCE

The tarragon in the lamb is mild, offering just a light hint of anise to the dish. The red-wine vinegar combined with the sugar and mint give the sauce its classic sweet-sour profile that works so well with the lamb.

Serves 8 to 10

FOR THE LAMB

3 tablespoons olive oil

½ cup dry red wine

1 tablespoon Dijon mustard

2 large cloves garlic, finely chopped
   (about 1 tablespoon)

3 tablespoons chopped fresh tarragon

Kosher salt and freshly ground
   black pepper

5 pounds boneless leg of lamb

FOR THE SAUCE

¼ cup olive oil

2 large cloves garlic, minced
   (about 1 tablespoon)

¼ cup red-wine vinegar, more to taste

2 teaspoons granulated sugar,
   more to taste

Freshly ground black pepper

1 bunch fresh mint, chopped (about 1 cup)

PREPARE & COOK THE LAMB

In a large non-reactive dish, mix 2 tablespoons oil with the wine, mustard, garlic, tarragon, 2 tablespoons salt, and 1 teaspoon black pepper. Add the lamb and coat with the marinade, cover, and refrigerate, flipping occasionally, for at least 8 hours and up to a day.

Position a rack in the center of the oven and heat the oven to 450°F. Put the lamb on a large cutting board and cut away any fatty patches. Set the lamb in a large roasting pan. Brush with the remaining tablespoon oil and sprinkle with pepper.

Roast the lamb until it starts to brown on top, 12 to 15 minutes. Reduce the oven's heat to 325°F and roast until an instant-read thermometer inserted into a thicker part of the lamb registers 135°F for medium-rare, 30 to 35 minutes. Transfer the lamb to a cutting board, tent with foil, and let rest for 10 minutes.

MAKE THE SAUCE

In a medium saucepan over medium heat, heat the oil with the garlic, stirring, until the garlic sizzles steadily and just starts to turn golden at the edges, about 2 minutes. Remove from the heat and add ¾ cup water and the vinegar. Whisk in the sugar until dissolved. Stir in ½ teaspoon pepper. Taste and season the sauce with more sugar, salt, and pepper if needed. Let sit at room temperature while the lamb roasts.

TO SERVE

Stir the mint into the sauce right before serving. Thinly
slice the lamb and serve with the mint sauce on the side.

GRILLED MOROCCAN
SPICE-CRUSTED LAMB
WITH SPICY CHILI SAUCE

Serve this grilled lamb with Mediterranean sides like saffron couscous and grilled zucchini and green and yellow bell peppers. Stuff any leftover lamb in a fresh pita with salad greens, tomatoes, and the chili sauce. The sauce is potent, so a little goes a long way.

Serves 4

FOR THE LAMB

Kosher salt

1 tablespoon light brown sugar

1 tablespoon ground cumin

1 tablespoon dried oregano

½ teaspoon ground cinnamon

½ teaspoon hot pimentón (smoked paprika) or chipotle powder

5 pounds boneless leg of lamb, trimmed

¼ cup chopped fresh cilantro

FOR THE SAUCE

¼ cup olive oil

1 large yellow onion, cut into ¼-inch dice (about 2 cups)

2 large jalapeño peppers (preferably red), cored, seeded, and finely diced (about ¼ cup)

Kosher salt

2 large cloves garlic, finely chopped (about 1 tablespoon)

2 teaspoons ground coriander

1 teaspoon ground cumin

½ teaspoon crushed red pepper flakes

2 tablespoons tomato paste

2 tablespoons white vinegar, more to taste

PREPARE THE LAMB

In a small bowl, mix 4 teaspoons salt with the sugar and spices. Sprinkle all over the lamb, transfer to a large non-reactive dish, and cover; refrigerate for at least 4 hours and up to 2 days.

MAKE THE SAUCE

Heat the oil in a medium (10-inch) sauté pan over medium heat until it's shimmering. Add the onion, jalapeños, and 1 teaspoon salt, and cook, stirring occasionally, until the onion softens and becomes translucent, about 8 minutes. Add the garlic, coriander, cumin, and red pepper flakes, and cook, stirring, until the garlic becomes fragrant, about 1 minute. Add the tomato paste, and cook, stirring, until the paste starts to darken, about 1 minute. Add ¾ cup water and the vinegar; bring to a boil, then simmer until the onion is completely tender, about 10 minutes. Transfer to a food processor and purée. Let cool to room temperature, season to taste with more salt, pepper, and vinegar if needed. Set aside; or transfer to an airtight container and refrigerate for up to three days.

GRILL THE LAMB

For a gas grill, light the front burner to medium-high and the back burner(s) to medium-low. For a charcoal grill, light a medium-hot fire (400°F) with two-thirds of the

continued

coals banked to one side. Clean and oil the grill grates. Grill the lamb over the hotter part of the fire without moving it until it's nicely browned, 6 to 8 minutes. Turn, move to the cooler part of the fire, and cook until an instant-read thermometer inserted into a thicker part of the lamb registers 135°F for medium-rare, 8 to 10 more minutes.

TO SERVE

Transfer the lamb to a cutting board, tent with foil, and let rest for 10 minutes. Thinly slice across the grain, transfer to a large platter, and sprinkle with the cilantro. Serve with the sauce on the side.

WHEN IT'S DONE

There are plenty of indicators used to check for doneness, but the best way to ensure you get your meat just to your liking is by taking its temperature with an instant-read thermometer. Just insert the thermometer in the thickest part of the meat, away from the bone.

DONENESS LEVEL	RECOMMENDED INTERNAL TEMP
Beef	
Rare	125°F
Medium-Rare	135°F
Medium	145°F
Medium-Well	155°F
Lamb	
Rare	125°F
Medium-Rare	135°F
Medium	145°F

 MAKE IT LAST Generally you'll find leg of lamb boneless and packed in Cryovac® at big buy stores. Try to cook it before its sell-by date, which is usually a couple weeks out from the date of purchase. In its packaging, the lamb will keep in the freezer for up to three months.

This luxury ingredient can now be an everyday indulgence, thanks to your big buy store. Paper thin and melt-in-your-mouth good, prosciutto is welcome in dishes both savory and sweet.

PROSCIUTTO

PROSCIUTTO-WRAPPED
HALIBUT WITH MUSHROOMS
& LEMON-ROSEMARY OIL

These fancy fish bundles are the perfect dish for company. You can assemble them a couple hours ahead and then slide them into the oven just before serving. Use a vegetable peeler to shave the lemon zest into strips.

Serves 4

6 tablespoons olive oil

Six 1-inch strips lemon zest

2 sprigs plus 1/2 teaspoon chopped
  fresh rosemary

1 3/4 pounds skinless halibut fillet,
  1- to 1 1/2-inch-thick, cut into 4 pieces

Kosher salt and freshly ground
  black pepper

3 1/2 ounces oyster mushrooms,
  broken into small pieces

8 thin slices prosciutto (about 4 ounces)

1 tablespoon freshly squeezed lemon juice

PROSCIUTTO PAIRINGS

Most are familiar with the classic combination of prosciutto and ripe melon, but this cured ham goes nicely in all sorts of other dishes:

• For a simple saltimbocca, sauté prosciutto with thin cutlets of chicken or veal, capers, and lemon juice.

• Wrap it around shrimp or scallops and then roast or grill.

• Thinly slice and sauté it with green vegetables like asparagus or broccoli.

Position a rack in the center of the oven, and heat the oven to 450°F.

Heat the oil, the lemon zest, and rosemary sprigs in a 2-quart saucepan over medium-low heat until the zest and rosemary sizzle and become very fragrant, about 2 minutes. Remove from the heat and let cool.

Brush the halibut with 2 tablespoons oil and sprinkle with 1/4 teaspoon salt and 1/2 teaspoon black pepper. In a small bowl, toss the mushrooms with 1 tablespoon oil, the chopped rosemary, and a pinch of salt. Arrange 2 slices of prosciutto on a cutting board so they overlap lengthwise. Top with a spoonful of the mushroom mixture and then a piece of the halibut. Wrap the prosciutto around the fish to form a bundle. Repeat with the remaining fish. Brush 2 tablespoons oil all over the bundles.

Set a rack over a large, rimmed baking sheet, and then transfer the fish bundles to the rack, seam side down. Roast the fish until it becomes firm to the touch and cooked through (use a paring knife to flake open a thick part to check) and the prosciutto browns, 13 to 15 minutes. Plate the fish bundles, whisk the remaining tablespoon oil with the lemon juice and drizzle over the fish. Serve immediately.

PENNE WITH CRISP PROSCIUTTO, ZUCCHINI & CORN

Sautéing the prosciutto in a skillet crisps and intensifies its texture and flavor so it becomes like a refined version of bacon. Instead of overpowering the dish, the prosciutto complements the sweetness of the corn, brightness of the mint, and delicate flavor of the zucchini.

Serves 4

Kosher salt

5 tablespoons olive oil

8 thin slices prosciutto (about 4 ounces), cut into strips

1 medium yellow onion, thinly sliced (1 cup)

2 small zucchini (about ¾ pound), trimmed, quartered lengthwise, and cut into 1½-inch pieces

2 ears corn, shucked and kernels sliced off (about 1 cup), or 1 cup frozen corn kernels, thawed

½ cup freshly grated Pecorino-Romano

3 tablespoons chopped fresh mint

1 pound penne

2 teaspoons sherry vinegar or cider vinegar

Freshly ground black pepper

Bring a large pot of well-salted water to a boil. Meanwhile, put 2 tablespoons oil and the prosciutto in a large (12-inch) skillet, place over medium heat, and cook, stirring occasionally, until the prosciutto browns in places and becomes crisp, about 5 minutes. Transfer the prosciutto to a large plate lined with paper towels.

Add 1 tablespoon oil and the onion to the skillet, sprinkle with ½ teaspoon salt, and cook, stirring occasionally, until the onion softens completely and turns light brown, about 6 minutes; add 1 or 2 tablespoons water to the skillet if the onion starts to stick or burn. Add the zucchini and corn, sprinkle with ¼ teaspoon salt, and cook, tossing occasionally, until the zucchini becomes tender, 4 to 5 minutes. Remove from the heat and stir in half the Pecorino-Romano and all the mint.

Add the penne to the pot of boiling water and cook according to the package directions. Reserve ½ cup of the pasta water and then drain the pasta. Add the pasta, the remaining 2 tablespoons oil, the vinegar, and 1 teaspoon black pepper to the skillet with the zucchini and corn mixture. Set the skillet over medium heat and cook, stirring, for 1 minute so the pasta mixes with the vegetables. Add the reserved pasta water and stir. Serve sprinkled with the crisp prosciutto and the remaining Pecorino-Romano.

In its original packaging, prosciutto will hold for at least three months. Once it's opened, treat prosciutto as you would other deli meats. Wrap it in waxed paper, refrigerate, and try to use it within three to four days.

ARUGULA, PROSCIUTTO & TOMATO PANINI

Dressing the arugula in oil and vinegar before assembling the sandwich enhances the peppery flavor of the greens and adds tang, much like an aïoli spread or tapenade would. Instead of Italian Fontina, try the Danish version of this cheese for a milder flavor and softer texture.

Serves 4

1 loosely packed cup baby arugula

3 tablespoons extra-virgin olive oil

1 teaspoon red-wine vinegar

Kosher salt and freshly ground
  black pepper

Eight ¾-inch-thick slices of rustic white
  bread (like ciabatta)

1 large clove garlic, halved

2 tomatoes, cored and cut into eight
  ½-inch-thick slices

8 thin slices prosciutto (about 4 ounces)

½ pound Danish Fontina, grated
  (about 2 cups)

In a medium bowl, toss the arugula with 1 tablespoon oil, the vinegar, ⅛ teaspoon salt, and ¼ teaspoon black pepper. Let sit for 5 minutes to wilt slightly. Set 4 slices of bread on a cutting board. Gently rub both sides of each piece of bread with the garlic. Top each slice of bread with 2 tomato slices and sprinkle evenly with ½ teaspoon salt. Layer the prosciutto, Fontina, and arugula mixture over the tomatoes. Rub both sides of the remaining 4 slices of bread with the garlic and set these slices, garlic-rubbed side down, on top of the arugula. Discard the garlic. Brush the outsides of the bread slices with the remaining 2 tablespoons oil.

Heat a panini press according to the manufacturer's instructions. (Alternatively, heat a nonstick grill pan over medium heat.) Put two of the sandwiches on the press, pull the top down, and cook until browned, 5 to 7 minutes. (If using a grill pan, put a heavy pan on top of the sandwiches and cook for roughly the same amount of time, turning the sandwiches over once.) Cook the remaining sandwiches in the same manner. Cut in half and serve.

The only problem with these mouthwatering ribs is they always leave you wanting more. But your local big buy store offers them in quantities large (and affordable) enough to ensure no one leaves the table hungry.

SPARERIBS

GRILLED SPARERIBS WITH MAPLE-CHIPOTLE GLAZE

Restraint and patience are the keys to grilling ribs properly. You want to put them over indirect heat (that is, over a cool zone) so the meat gently cooks. Make sure to cover the grill so that the ribs' flavor is enhanced with a healthy waft of smoke.

Serves 4

FOR THE RIBS

1 tablespoon granulated sugar

1 tablespoon chili powder

½ teaspoon ground cumin

Kosher salt and freshly ground
   black pepper

2 racks pork spareribs (about 9 pounds)

FOR THE GLAZE

¾ cup pure maple syrup

1 chipotle chile, chopped,
   plus 3 tablespoons adobo sauce
   (from a can of chipotles en adobo)

2 tablespoons ketchup

1½ tablespoons Dijon mustard

1 tablespoon cider vinegar

PREPARE & COOK THE RIBS

For a gas grill, light the front burner to medium-low and leave the back burner(s) off. For a charcoal grill, light a medium fire (300°F to 350°F) with all the coals banked to one side and the other side empty. Clean and oil the grill grates.

In a small bowl, mix the sugar and spices with 4 teaspoons salt and 1 teaspoon pepper, and pat over both sides of the ribs. Let sit at room temperature while the grill heats.

Set the ribs meaty side up over the cool zone of the fire and cook covered (with the vents open on a charcoal grill) until the ribs brown and become tender (a paring knife should easily slice into the meat and the ribs should sag if you hold the center up with a pair of tongs), about 1½ hours.

MAKE THE GLAZE

Stir together the maple syrup, chipotle chile and adobo sauce, ketchup, mustard, and vinegar in a medium bowl until combined. Brush the ribs with half the glaze and cook with the grill covered, brushing the meat every couple minutes, until the glaze browns and becomes sticky on the ribs, about 15 minutes. Remove the ribs from the grill, brush with the remaining glaze, and let cool for a couple minutes; cut in half (meaty side down so they're easier to slice), and serve.

SPANISH SPARERIBS
WITH HERB-GARLIC DIPPING SAUCE

This popular Spanish dish is simple but wonderful. Serve the ribs as a hearty appetizer with plenty of napkins or as a main course with sautéed greens and chickpeas. Use good-quality dried oregano in the sauce and add some diced roasted red pepper (especially Spanish piquillos) if you have them on hand.

Serves 4 as a main course or 12 as an appetizer

FOR THE RIBS
Kosher salt and freshly ground
   black pepper
2 teaspoons hot pimentón (smoked
   paprika) or ½ teaspoon cayenne
2 teaspoons dried oregano
2 teaspoons granulated sugar
2 racks pork spareribs (about 9 pounds)

FOR THE SAUCE
6 tablespoons sherry vinegar or
   white-wine vinegar
4 large cloves garlic, minced
   (about 1 tablespoon)
1 tablespoon dried oregano
¼ cup extra-virgin olive oil
Kosher salt

GRILL THE RIBS
Clean and oil the grill grates. For a gas grill, light the front burner to medium low and leave the back burner(s) off. For a charcoal grill, light a medium fire (300°F to 350°F) with all the coals banked to one side and the other side empty.

In a small bowl, mix 2 tablespoons salt with 2 teaspoons pepper with the pimentón or cayenne, oregano, and sugar. Pat the mixture all over both sides of the ribs. Let sit at room temperature while the grill heats.

Set the ribs, meaty side up, over the cool zone of the fire and cook covered (with the vents open on a charcoal grill) until the ribs brown and become tender (a paring knife should easily slice into the meat and the ribs should sag if you hold the center up with a pair of tongs), about 1½ hours.

MAKE THE SAUCE
While the ribs cook, combine 2 tablespoons vinegar with the garlic and oregano in a medium bowl. Using the bottom of a small spoon, smash the garlic and oregano against the bottom and sides of the bowl until it turns into a paste with the vinegar. Whisk in the remaining vinegar, ⅓ cup water, the oil, and 2 teaspoons salt.

Transfer the ribs to a carving board to rest for 5 minutes. Cut the racks (meaty side down so they're easier to slice) into individual ribs and transfer to a plate. Whisk the sauce well, drizzle on top of the ribs, and serve.

MAKE IT LAST Spareribs in big buy stores typically come in vacuum packs with a sell-by date a couple weeks out. Unopened, the vacuum-packed sealed ribs should keep in the freezer for about two months. After opening the packs, wrap unused portions of ribs in a few layers of aluminum foil and then in a zip-top bag, or vacuum-seal them in bags if you have the proper equipment, and stow them in the freezer. Uncooked racks kept in the refrigerator should be used within one to two days.

ROASTED TERIYAKI
SPARERIBS

A low oven gently roasts these ribs to a moist and tender doneness. The sweet-salty teriyaki glaze goes well with steamed rice and stir-fried vegetables.

Serves 4

FOR THE RIBS

2 racks pork spareribs (about 9 pounds)

2 tablespoons light brown sugar

Kosher salt

1 tablespoon Asian sesame oil

2 teaspoons five-spice powder

FOR THE GLAZE

¼ cup peeled and coarsely chopped
fresh ginger

2 medium cloves garlic, coarsely chopped

2 tablespoons canola oil

½ cup honey

¼ cup reduced-sodium soy sauce

2 tablespoons white vinegar

1 tablespoon Asian sesame oil

2 teaspoons toasted sesame seeds (see
Toasting Nuts, p. 41)

1 teaspoon Asian chili sauce (like Sriracha)

2 teaspoons cornstarch

PREPARE & COOK THE RIBS

Position a rack in the center of the oven. Heat the oven to 325°F. Line a rimmed baking sheet with aluminum foil, and place a cooking rack on top of the foil. In a small bowl, mix the brown sugar, 1 tablespoon salt, the sesame oil, and 5-spice powder, and rub over the ribs. Arrange the ribs meaty side up on the rack. Roast until the ribs brown and become tender, about 2 hours.

MAKE THE GLAZE

Put the ginger and garlic in a mini chopper or food processor and process until minced. In a small (2-quart) saucepan, combine the canola oil, garlic, and ginger, and cook over medium heat, stirring occasionally, until the mixture becomes very fragrant and the garlic and ginger start to brown lightly, about 2½ minutes. Add the honey, soy sauce, vinegar, sesame oil, sesame seeds, and chili sauce, and bring to a simmer. Whisk the cornstarch with 2 tablespoons water and stir into the honey mixture. Cook the sauce, stirring, until it thickens, about 1 minute. Remove from the heat. Divide the glaze between two bowls, and set one bowl aside.

Raise the oven temperature to 425°F. Brush the ribs with one bowl of the glaze and continue to roast, brushing every couple minutes, until the glaze browns and caramelizes, about 10 minutes total. Remove from the oven and let cool for a couple minutes, then transfer the ribs to a cutting board and cut the racks in half (meaty side down so they're easier to slice). Serve with the remaining glaze for dipping.

Because it is less fatty than rib eye, more flavorful than filet mignon, and reasonably priced, bringing home a whole top loin is pure genius. Cut into steaks and get cooking.

BEEF
TOP LOIN

PAN-SEARED STEAK WITH ITALIAN-STYLE SALSA VERDE

Italian salsa verde is a lively herb paste that adds zest to grilled and roasted meats. Heap any leftover steak on a hoagie roll for a delicious sandwich.

Serves 4

Four ¾-inch-thick top loin (New York strip) steaks (8 to 10 ounces each), trimmed
1 teaspoon chopped fresh thyme
Kosher salt and freshly ground black pepper
1½ cups chopped fresh flat-leaf parsley
½ cup plus 2 tablespoons extra-virgin olive oil
½ cup chopped cornichons or small sour gherkins
2 tablespoons fresh lemon juice, more to taste
2 tablespoons capers, rinsed and drained
1 large clove garlic, minced and mashed to a paste

Put the steaks on a large plate and sprinkle both sides with the thyme, 1½ teaspoons salt, and ½ teaspoon black pepper.

In a food processor, combine the parsley, ½ cup of the extra-virgin olive oil, the cornichons, lemon juice, capers, garlic, ½ teaspoon salt, and 1 teaspoon black pepper; process until smooth. Taste and add more lemon juice, salt, or pepper if needed.

Heat the remaining 2 tablespoons olive oil in a large (12-inch) sauté pan over medium-high heat. Add the steaks and cook without touching until they brown, about 2 minutes. Turn and cook until the second side browns; for medium-rare, the steaks should be light pink when you slice into a thicker part, and an instant-read thermometer should read 135°F, about 2 to 3 additional minutes. (See When It's Done, p. 106, for meat temperature guidelines.) Let the steaks rest for 3 to 5 minutes before serving with the salsa verde.

TRIMMING AND PORTIONING

A steak from a beef top loin is called a New York strip steak. To trim and portion the loin into steaks, start by trimming about ¼ inch of the fat cap running along its top side with a sharp boning knife. Use a chef's knife to cut the trimmed loin into steaks. Cut the steaks between 1 and 1½ inches thick, depending on how you will cook them, which will yield 8- to 14-ounce steaks.

prep this

SEAR-ROASTED ROSEMARY STEAK & POTATOES

This is a one-pan take on steak and potatoes. Sear the steaks on the stovetop, and then roast them with small red potatoes and rosemary sprigs. Thinly slice the beef and serve with the potatoes and balsamic-glazed Brussels sprouts or roasted asparagus.

Serves 4

Four 1½-inch-thick top loin (New York strip) steaks (8 to 10 ounces each), trimmed
1 teaspoon chopped fresh rosemary plus 3 sprigs, pulled apart into smaller pieces
Kosher salt and freshly ground black pepper
3 tablespoons unsalted butter
2 tablespoons olive oil
1½ pounds small red potatoes, halved or quartered if large
2 teaspoons balsamic vinegar

MATCH THICKNESS TO COOKING METHOD
When buying a whole top loin, you can choose the thickness of the strip steaks to suit your preferences and the preparation. Thin steaks (about ¾ inch thick) are great for pan-frying quickly on the stovetop. Thicker steaks (about 1½ inches thick), the preference of most meat-lovers, can be seared on the stovetop, but are then best finished in the oven so they slowly cook through (and don't smoke up the whole kitchen). Steaks somewhere in the middle (about 1 inch thick) are perfect for medium-high heat on the grill.

Position a rack in the center of the oven and heat the oven to 425°F. Sprinkle the steaks with the chopped rosemary, 1½ teaspoons salt, and ¾ teaspoon pepper. In a large (12-inch), oven-proof, heavy-duty skillet (like a cast-iron pan) over medium-high heat, combine 1 tablespoon each of the butter and oil and heat until the butter melts and its foam subsides. Add the steaks and cook without touching until they brown around the edges and easily release from the pan, about 3 minutes. Flip and cook the other sides until they brown, about 2 minutes. Transfer to a large plate.

Add the remaining 1 tablespoon oil to the skillet. Arrange the potatoes, cut side down, in the skillet, scatter the rosemary leaves around the potatoes, sprinkle with ½ teaspoon salt, and transfer to the oven. Roast until the potatoes are tender when pierced, about 15 minutes. Set the steaks atop the potatoes and cook until the steaks are medium-rare—an instant-read thermometer inserted into the thickest part should register 135°F, about 10 minutes.

Transfer the steaks to a cutting board and let rest for 5 minutes. Toss the potatoes with the remaining 2 tablespoons butter and the balsamic vinegar, and keep warm in the oven (turn the oven off and leave the door slightly open). Serve the steaks thinly sliced, with the potatoes on the side, drizzled with any remaining balsamic and butter mixture and sprinkled lightly with salt and pepper.

MAKE IT LAST Once a top loin has been removed from its packaging, keep it whole and it will last longer, three to five days. With cut steaks, spoilage occurs at a faster rate, so use the meat within one to two days' time and store portioned steaks in parchment or waxed paper for ease of handling and storage. Beef starts to discolor and spoil after any longer than this. If you decide to freeze any or all of the loin, vacuum-seal it in bags if you have the proper equipment, and stow it in the freezer for up to three months.

MARINATED STEAK
WITH GRILLED SCALLIONS

The intense flavor of this homemade marinade adds a special touch to these fine steaks. The grilled scallions make a perfect accompaniment to the beef.

Serves 4

Four 1-inch-thick top loin (New York strip) steaks (8 to 10 ounces each), trimmed
Kosher salt and freshly ground black pepper
5 tablespoons canola oil
2 tablespoons reduced-sodium soy sauce
4 teaspoons chopped fresh thyme
1 tablespoon Worcestershire sauce
1 tablespoon Dijon mustard
1 tablespoon red-wine vinegar
1 large clove garlic, minced
10 scallions, bulbs split in half lengthwise if large

LET THEM SIT

The goal when searing steaks is to brown the outside but keep the inside nice and pink. Letting beef sit at room temperature for about 30 minutes before sautéing or grilling helps with this process by allowing the interior of the meat to warm a bit so it hits the desired medium or medium-rare temperature more quickly, which, in turn, avoids charring the outside while undercooking the interior.

Sprinkle the steaks with 1¼ teaspoons salt and 2 teaspoons pepper.

In a medium bowl, mix 4 tablespoons oil with the soy sauce, 3 teaspoons thyme, the Worcestershire, mustard, vinegar, and garlic. Put the steaks in a large bowl and coat them with the soy sauce mixture. Cover the bowl and marinate the steaks in the refrigerator, turning occasionally, for at least 4 hours and up to 1 day.

For a gas grill, light the front burner to medium-high and the back burner(s) to medium-low. For a charcoal grill, light a medium fire (about 300°F to 350°F) with two-thirds of the coals banked to one side. Clean and oil the grill grates. While the grill heats, set the steaks out at room temperature. Toss the scallions with the remaining tablespoon oil and ½ teaspoon each salt and pepper.

Set the steaks over the hotter part of the fire and the scallions over the cooler zone. Cook, covered, until the scallions brown, about 3 minutes, and the steaks have good grill marks and easily release from the grate, about 4 minutes. Flip both the scallions and steaks. Cook the steaks until they're just firm to the touch, pink when you slice into a thicker part, and register 135°F on an instant-read thermometer for medium-rare, about 4 minutes. Grill the scallions until browned and softened, about 3 more minutes.

Transfer the steaks to dinner plates, top with the remaining teaspoon thyme, and serve with the scallions.

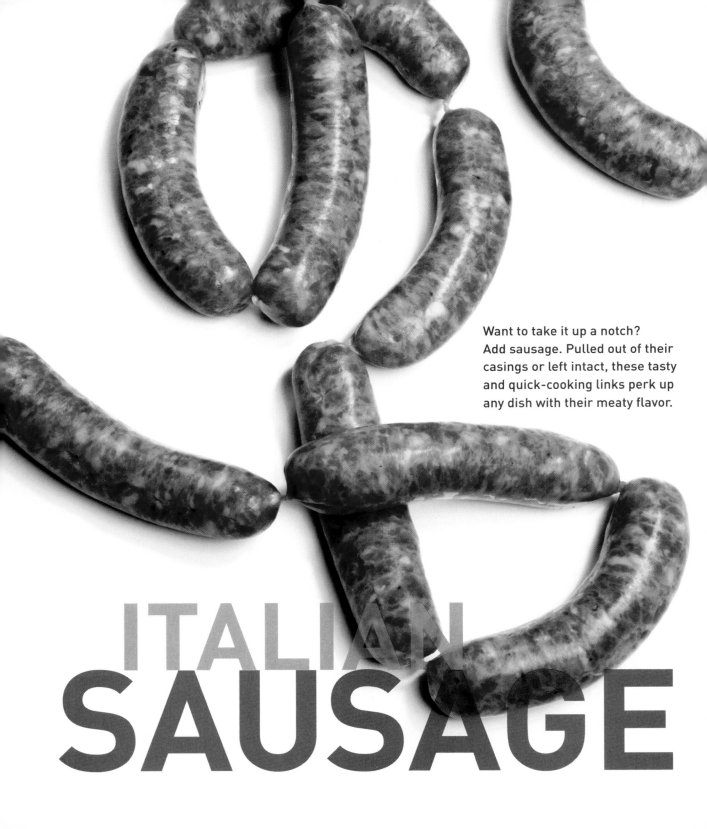

Want to take it up a notch? Add sausage. Pulled out of their casings or left intact, these tasty and quick-cooking links perk up any dish with their meaty flavor.

ITALIAN SAUSAGE

GRILLED SAUSAGE & EGGPLANT PARMIGIANO PIZZA

Grilling these pizzas gives the crust a wonderfully crisp texture, and the sausage and eggplant get a smoky edge. It's easy enough to make the dough yourself, though you can use store-bought (about ¾ pound for both pizzas) if you're pressed for time. When prepping the eggplant, leave the skin intact so the peeled eggplant won't fall apart on the grill.

Serves 6 to 8

FOR THE DOUGH

1 teaspoon active dry yeast

¼ teaspoon granulated sugar

9 ounces (2 cups) unbleached all-purpose flour, more as needed

1 tablespoon olive oil, more for the bowl

Kosher salt

FOR THE PIZZA

1 small eggplant (about ½ pound), trimmed and cut into ¼-inch-thick slices

7 tablespoons olive oil

Kosher salt

2 links (½ pound) sweet Italian sausage

2 large tomatoes, chopped (about 2 cups)

2 teaspoons chopped fresh thyme

Freshly ground black pepper

6 ounces fresh mozzarella, thinly sliced

¼ cup freshly grated Parmigiano-Reggiano

¼ cup basil leaves, thinly sliced

MAKE THE DOUGH

Mix ¾ cup of warm water (between 100°F and 110°F) with the yeast and sugar in a 1-cup measure, and let sit for 5 to 10 minutes, until the surface of the liquid becomes frothy. In a stand mixer fitted with a dough hook, mix the flour, 1 tablespoon oil, and 1 teaspoon salt on low speed until combined. Add the yeast mixture and continue mixing, scraping down the sides of the bowl as necessary, until a dough forms, about 3 minutes. Add 1 or 2 tablespoons of water or flour if the dough is too dry or wet, respectively. Transfer the dough to a floured work surface and knead until it becomes smooth and elastic, about 5 minutes. Transfer to a large oiled bowl, cover with a dishtowel, and let sit at room temperature until the dough almost doubles in size, 1 to 2 hours. (The dough can be made up to 2 days ahead and refrigerated in a zip-top plastic bag.)

MAKE THE PIZZAS

For a gas grill heat the back burner(s) to medium-high and the front burner to low. For a charcoal grill, light a large fire and push the coals to one side of the grill; the fire is ready when you can hold your hand a couple inches above the hot zone for just 3 to 4 seconds. Clean and oil the grill grates. Brush both sides of the eggplant slices

continued

with 2 tablespoons oil, sprinkle with ½ teaspoon salt, and grill over the hot part of the fire along with the sausage, flipping occasionally, until the eggplant is completely tender, about 8 minutes, and the sausage is cooked through, 10 to 12 minutes. Let cool for a couple minutes and then thinly slice the sausage. In a medium bowl, mix the tomatoes with the thyme, ¼ teaspoon salt, and ½ teaspoon black pepper.

Line two baking sheets with parchment paper. Form the dough into 2 equal balls and transfer to a floured work surface. Shape each into a thin round, 10 to 12 inches wide. Brush the top side with 1 tablespoon oil then flip the oiled side over onto the prepared baking sheet. Brush the other side with 1 tablespoon oil and cover with a piece of parchment paper. Repeat with the second ball of dough and the second baking sheet. (You can grill the pizzas immediately or hold at room temperature for up to 1 hour.)

When you are ready to grill, peel back the parchment on top of one dough round. With two hands, support the dough under the remaining parchment paper side, flip it dough side down onto the grill's hot zone, and peel off the parchment paper from the facing side. Cook the dough without moving until it bubbles and gets good grill marks, about 1 minute. Rotate it 90° and cook until the dough is uniformly browned but not burnt, about 30 seconds to 1 minute. Pull the dough to the cooler zone of the charcoal fire or to the front of the gas grill and reduce the middle zone's heat to medium-low. Flip the dough and top evenly with half of the tomatoes, sausage, eggplant, mozzarella, Parmigiano-Reggiano, a drizzle of the remaining tablespoon of oil, and a light sprinkling of salt. Cover the grill (with the vents open on a charcoal grill) and cook, rotating the pizza about every minute until it cooks evenly and the cheese melts, about 3 to 5 minutes. Sprinkle with the basil, transfer to a large cutting board, slice, and tent with aluminum foil while cooking the second pizza. Grill and top the remaining pizza in the same manner, and serve.

MAKE IT LAST Keep sausage on hand to add salty, meaty flavor to dishes. Most sausage will hold fine in the refrigerator for three or four days after opening. For longer storage, pack a couple of links in a zip-top bag and put them in the freezer, where they'll keep for up to three months. When ready to use them, simply pull a few sausages out at a time, and allow them to thaw safely in the fridge.

left: grilled **sausage** & eggplant parmigiano pizza

CLAMS & SAUSAGE
IN A SPICY TOMATO-JALAPEÑO BROTH

If you're a heat fiend, adding a second jalapeño to this braise gives it some real fire. The addition of kale or spinach to the broth would make this dish even heartier. Serve over pasta or with a fresh, crusty baguette.

Serves 4

3 tablespoons olive oil

4 links (about 1 pound) sweet Italian sausage, casings removed and broken into 1-inch pieces

1 large bulb fennel, trimmed, cored, and cut into ½-inch dice (4 cups)

Kosher salt and freshly ground black pepper

1 jalapeño pepper, cored, seeded, and chopped (about 2 tablespoons)

2 medium cloves garlic, chopped

1 teaspoon chopped fresh rosemary

½ cup dry white wine

One 28-ounce can diced tomatoes and their juices (3 cups), puréed

2 pounds littleneck clams (about 16), scrubbed and rinsed of any grit

12 basil leaves, torn into small pieces

Heat 2 tablespoons oil in a large Dutch oven over medium heat for 1 minute. Add the sausage and cook until the sausage browns and loses its raw color, about 6 minutes. Transfer to a large plate.

Add the remaining tablespoon oil and the fennel, sprinkle with ½ teaspoon salt and ¼ teaspoon pepper, and cook, stirring, until the fennel starts to soften and brown lightly, about 4 minutes. Add the jalapeño, garlic, and rosemary, and cook, stirring, until the garlic becomes fragrant, about 30 seconds.

Add the white wine, and then raise the heat to high and cook, stirring to pick up any browned bits on the bottom of the pan, until the wine almost completely reduces, about 2 minutes. Return the sausage to the pot along with the tomatoes (and their juices), ½ teaspoon salt, and ½ teaspoon pepper, and reduce the heat to a simmer. Cook the sausage, stirring occasionally, until it cooks through, about 10 minutes. Taste and season the broth with more salt and pepper if needed.

Add the clams and half the basil. Raise the heat to medium high and cover the pot. Cook the clams, shaking the pot occasionally, until they all open, about 4 minutes. Discard any clams that don't open. Remove from the heat, ladle into 4 bowls, and serve sprinkled with the remaining basil.

BRAISED SAUSAGE
WITH BALSAMIC-GLAZED ONIONS & GRAPES

Sausage and grapes are a classic Italian pairing. The addition of balsamic vinegar and caramelized onions turns this into a quick, warming braise. Piercing the sausages with the tines of a fork will allow them to release some of their juices and infuse the broth. Serve with a crusty baguette and a green salad.

Serves 4

3 tablespoons olive oil

8 links sweet Italian sausage
  (about 2 pounds), pricked with a fork

1 large yellow onion, thinly sliced
  (about 2 cups)

Kosher salt

1/2 cup lower-salt chicken broth

2 tablespoons balsamic vinegar

20 seedless red grapes, halved

2 tablespoons chopped fresh oregano

VERSATILE LINKS

Like bacon, sausage is a great ingredient to have on hand to mix with vegetables, soups, stews, and pastas. Break it up into crumbled pieces and keep in small zip-top bags in the freezer to pull out at a moment's notice to add richness to a number of dishes: in sautéed broccoli, in a creamy pasta sauce with caramelized onions and mushrooms, or in a white bean soup with rosemary.

Heat 1 tablespoon oil in a large (12-inch) skillet over medium heat until it's shimmering. Add the sausages and cook, turning every couple minutes, until they're browned all over, about 8 minutes. Transfer to a large plate.

Add the remaining 2 tablespoons oil and the onion to the pot, sprinkle with 1/2 teaspoon salt, and cook, stirring occasionally, until the onion softens completely and starts to turn light brown, about 7 minutes. Add the chicken broth and balsamic vinegar, and scrape the bottom of the pot with a wooden spoon to incorporate any browned bits. Reduce to a gentle simmer (medium-low or low depending on your stovetop). Add the sausages and grapes, cover the pot with the lid ajar, and cook, stirring occasionally, until the sausages are cooked through (slice into one to check), about 25 minutes. Serve sprinkled with the oregano.

SALMON

Rich and fatty, salmon readily absorbs flavor and is most forgiving when it comes to overcooking. It's a bit of a world traveller, too—inspiring Mexican, Mediterranean, and Asian dishes.

BROILED SALMON
WITH GINGER-SHIITAKE GLAZE

Though most glazes are applied with a brush, this slightly chunky mixture of sautéed mushrooms and red peppers is spooned over the fish. The honey helps the crust brown, and a splash of vinegar and a spoonful of chili paste perk up the fish, while the vegetables add texture and color.

Serves 4

2 pounds salmon fillet, skin on

3 tablespoons canola oil, more for the baking sheet

¼ teaspoon ground coriander

Kosher salt and freshly ground black pepper

½ small red bell pepper, finely diced (about ¼ cup)

3 scallions, trimmed and thinly sliced (white and green parts separated)

2 tablespoons finely chopped ginger

3½ ounces shiitake mushrooms, stemmed and cut into ¼-inch dice (about 1 cup)

¼ cup honey

3 tablespoons rice vinegar

1 tablespoon reduced-sodium soy sauce

1 teaspoon Asian chili sauce (like Sriracha)

1 teaspoon cornstarch

Position an oven rack about 8 inches away from the broiler element and heat the broiler to high.

Oil a large, rimmed baking sheet. Set the salmon skin side down on the baking sheet, sprinkle with 1 tablespoon oil, the coriander, ½ teaspoon salt, and ½ teaspoon pepper, and let sit at room temperature while you prepare the sauce.

In a large (12-inch) skillet over medium-high heat, cook the red pepper, scallion whites, and ginger in the remaining 2 tablespoons oil, stirring occasionally, until the red pepper and scallions start to soften and brown, about 3 minutes. Add the mushrooms, raise the heat to medium high, sprinkle with ¼ teaspoon salt, and cook, stirring, until they soften and start to brown, about 3 minutes. Add the honey, vinegar, soy sauce, chili sauce, and ¼ cup water, and bring to a simmer. Whisk the cornstarch with 1 teaspoon water and stir into the glaze. Return to a simmer and cook until the glaze thickens, about 1 minute. Remove from the heat.

Broil the salmon until it starts to brown and becomes almost firm to the touch, about 8 minutes. Momentarily

continued

transfer to the stovetop and spoon the glaze over the salmon. Return to the oven and broil for about 1 more minute so the glaze browns and the salmon almost completely cooks through (check by using a paring knife to flake a thicker part of the fillet). Sprinkle with the scallion greens, transfer to a large platter, and serve.

SKINNING SALMON

Though butchering fish can be complicated work, skinning salmon is quite simple. Make a little slice at one corner of the fillet a couple inches wide, separating the skin from the flesh of the salmon. Then with one hand holding the knife at a 30-degree angle and the other holding the corner of skin, firmly pull on the skin while slicing the knife back and forth (the skin hand will do most of the work) so the skin pulls free.

Skinning grilled salmon is just as easy. Grill the salmon fillet, but before removing the salmon from the grill, slip a spatula between the skin and the flesh, leaving the skin behind. By the time the grill is cool the skin will have become ash and can be brushed off the grate.

prep this

left: broiled **salmon** with ginger-shiitake glaze

ROAST SALMON
WITH BACON & LEEKS

Crisp bacon and sautéed leeks complement salmon's rich, full flavor. Serve with roasted fingerling potatoes or herbed couscous. If entertaining, you can cook and serve the fillet whole.

Serves 4

2 pounds salmon fillet, skin on,
  cut into four 8-ounce pieces
3 tablespoons olive oil
2 teaspoons chopped fresh thyme
Kosher salt and freshly ground
  black pepper
¼ pound thickly sliced bacon,
  cut crosswise into thin strips
1 large leek (white and light green parts
  only), trimmed and thinly sliced crosswise into rings (2 cups)
2 teaspoons cider vinegar

Position the rack in the center of the oven and heat the oven to 400°F. Rub the salmon flesh with 1 tablespoon oil and then sprinkle with half the thyme, ¾ teaspoon salt, and ½ teaspoon pepper.

In a large (12-inch), oven-proof skillet (like a cast-iron pan) over medium heat, cook the bacon in 1 tablespoon oil, stirring occasionally, until it crisps and renders most of its fat, about 5 minutes. Transfer to a plate lined with paper towels. Discard the bacon fat and wipe the pan with a paper towel.

Add the remaining tablespoon oil and the leek to the pan, sprinkle with ½ teaspoon salt, the remaining thyme, and the vinegar, and cook over low heat, stirring occasionally, until the leek softens completely and turns light brown, about 10 minutes.

Spread the leeks evenly around the pan and set the salmon skin side down on top. Transfer to the oven and roast uncovered until the salmon browns and becomes mostly firm to the touch (it should be just a little pink inside when you flake open a thicker piece of the fish), about 20 minutes.

Serve the salmon with leeks and crisp bacon on top.

MAKE IT LAST Salmon should stay fresh in the refrigerator for one to two days; do make sure to check the sell-by date before purchasing. Freezing fresh salmon at home isn't recommended. Home freezers can't do as good a job preserving the fish as industrial freezers and can compromise the texture of the fish.

SALMON BURGERS
WITH DILL TARTAR SAUCE

To make these burgers, "grind" the salmon fillet by pulsing it in a food processor. Make sure the fish is chilled so it chops easily. Because the burgers are somewhat loosely packed, it's easier to sear them on the stovetop than on the grill (where they are more inclined to fall apart).

Serves 4

1½ pounds salmon fillet, skinned,
   cut into 1-inch cubes, and chilled
1 small shallot, finely diced
   (about 2 tablespoons)
1 tablespoon capers, rinsed and chopped
1 teaspoon Dijon mustard
Kosher salt and freshly ground
   black pepper
½ cup mayonnaise
⅓ cup dill pickle relish
2 tablespoons chopped fresh dill
2 tablespoons fresh lemon juice,
   more to taste
2 tablespoons olive oil
1 cup lightly packed baby spinach
   (about 1 ounce)
1 small red onion, cut into thin rings
1 large tomato, cut into 8 thin slices
4 hamburger buns, split and toasted

Put half of the salmon in a food processor and pulse until it's coarsely chopped. Transfer to a medium bowl. Chop the remaining salmon in the same manner, and add to the bowl. Fold in the shallot, capers, mustard, and ¾ teaspoon each salt and pepper. Form into four ¾-inch-thick patties, set on a large oiled plate and cover, and refrigerate until ready to cook (up to 4 hours).

Meanwhile, make the tartar sauce. In a small bowl, mix the mayonnaise with the relish, dill, lemon juice, and ¼ teaspoon each salt and pepper. Taste and add more lemon juice, salt, and pepper if needed. The sauce will keep for up to one day in the refrigerator.

Heat the oil in a large (12-inch), nonstick skillet over medium-high heat until it's shimmering. Add the salmon burgers (straight from the refrigerator; the cold temperature will help them hold together), reduce the heat to medium, and cook without touching until they brown at the edges, 2 to 3 minutes. Flip and cook the other sides until they, too, are browned and the burgers are just a little pink in the center (check by slicing into a thicker part of one of the burgers with a paring knife), about 3 to 4 more minutes.

Put the spinach, onion, and 2 tomato slices on each of the buns; top with the burgers and a dollop of the tartar sauce; add the top of the bun and serve.

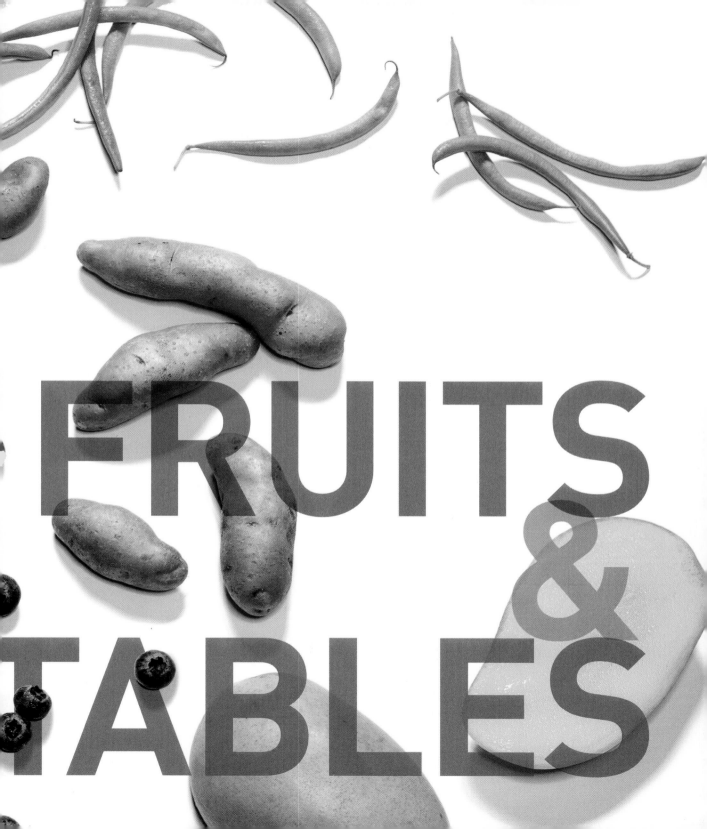

FRUITS
&
TABLES

FRUITS & VEGETABLES

AVOCADOS

With its buttery, creamy goodness, one avocado is never enough. Great in dips, spreads, sandwiches, this is one big buy ingredient you'll come back to time and again.

SUMMERY AVOCADO BLTS

These sandwiches are wonderful as is, though you can certainly layer on some sliced turkey or sharp Cheddar if you like. Pick up the best ingredients—a juicy heirloom tomato, fresh lettuce, and good-quality bacon—to ensure the best flavor in this classic sandwich.

Serves 4

2 large Haas avocados (about 1 pound)
1 tablespoon fresh lemon juice,
  more to taste
Kosher salt
1 large tomato (about ¾ pound), 8 slices
2 tablespoons olive oil
8 thick slices bacon (about 10 ounces)
1 large Vidalia onion, cut into
  ½-inch-thick rounds (about 8 rounds)
Eight ½-inch-thick slices bread
  (rustic white, whole wheat,
  or sourdough), toasted
8 Boston lettuce leaves

In a small bowl, mash one of the avocados with the lemon juice and ¼ teaspoon salt. Taste and season the avocado with more lemon juice and salt if needed. Slice the second avocado into thin slices. Fan the tomato slices on a large plate, drizzle with 1 tablespoon oil, and sprinkle with ½ teaspoon salt.

In a large (12-inch), heavy-duty skillet (like cast-iron), cook the bacon with the remaining 1 tablespoon oil over medium heat, flipping occasionally, until it browns and renders much of its fat, about 5 minutes. Transfer the bacon to a plate lined with paper towels. Add the onion rounds to the skillet, sprinkle lightly with salt, and cook until they start to brown, about 2 minutes. Flip and cook until the other sides brown but they are still firm, about 2 more minutes. Remove from the heat.

For each sandwich, spread the mashed avocado on one bread slice. Top with 2 slices of tomato, 2 onion rounds, bacon, lettuce, and avocado slices. Add the remaining slice of bread, and serve.

PITTING AVOCADOS

Using a chef's knife, split the avocado in half lengthwise. The pit will be stuck in one of the halves. Carefully and gently tap the pit with the knife blade so that the blade notches into the pit. Rotate the avocado half so the pit twists free.

prep
this

SPICY CHIPOTLE SHRIMP, AVOCADO & CORN FAJITAS

To heat the corn tortillas but keep them from ripping or cracking, warm them in a nonstick skillet over medium-low heat, 10 to 15 seconds on each side, and then put them between layers of damp paper towels until they are ready to be served. Arrange the fajitas and fixings on a buffet table, bar style, for casual entertaining, or serve the components on various platters at the table.

Serves 4

1 pound shrimp (26 to 30 per pound), peeled and deveined

4 tablespoons olive oil

1 teaspoon chili powder

Kosher salt and freshly ground black pepper

1 large Haas avocado (about ½ pound), cut into ½-inch dice

1 chipotle, minced, plus 1 tablespoon adobo sauce (from a can of chipotles en adobo)

1 lime, half juiced (about 1 tablespoon) and half cut into wedges

1 large yellow onion, thinly sliced (about 3 cups)

1 large clove garlic, minced

1 cup frozen corn, thawed, or the kernels from 2 ears corn

8 corn tortillas, warmed

¼ cup coarsely chopped fresh cilantro

Toss the shrimp with 1 tablespoon oil, the chili powder, ¼ teaspoon salt, and ½ teaspoon pepper. In a medium bowl, mash the avocado with the chipotle and adobo sauce, lime juice, and ¼ teaspoon salt.

Heat 1½ tablespoons oil in a large (12-inch) skillet over medium-high heat until shimmering. Add the shrimp and cook, stirring, until they turn pink and become just firm to the touch, about 2 minutes. Transfer to a large plate.

Reduce the heat to medium, and add the remaining 1½ tablespoons oil to the pan. Add the onion, sprinkle with ½ teaspoon salt, and cook, stirring, until the onion softens and starts to brown, about 6 minutes. Add the garlic and cook, stirring, for 30 seconds. Add the corn and shrimp, and cook, stirring, until they heat through, about 2 minutes.

Let your guests help themselves by spreading the avocado on a warm tortilla and topping the spread with some of the shrimp mixture, a squeeze of lime juice, and a sprinkling of the cilantro.

CHUNKY
GUACAMOLE

There are few dishes as simple yet easily varied as guacamole. This version lets the flavor and texture of the avocado shine through, amply reinforced with cilantro, red onion, and a splash of lime juice. It can be set out as a dip, used as a garnish for tacos or chili, or spread on sandwiches and burgers.

Makes 2½ cups

1 medium tomato, finely diced (about 1 cup)

½ small red onion, finely diced
(about 3 tablespoons)

½ cup coarsely chopped fresh cilantro

3 tablespoons fresh lime juice

¼ teaspoon crushed red pepper flakes

Kosher salt

2 large Haas avocados (about 1 pound),
cut into ½-inch dice

In a medium bowl, toss the tomatoes with the onion, cilantro, lime juice, red pepper flakes, and 1 teaspoon salt, and let sit for about 5 minutes. Add the avocado and gently mash it into the tomato mixture with a fork. Serve immediately.

MAKE IT LAST Store avocados at room temperature until they just become soft and ripe, and then transfer them to the refrigerator where they'll keep for up to one week. (Their skin darkens as the avocados become ripe.) If you want avocados to ripen quickly, put them in a brown paper bag and store them in a warm place (such as near the stove) for a day or two.

Slender and springtime green, haricots verts have a tender, delicate flavor and look pretty on the plate. Delectable both cooked and raw—just wash, trim, and go.

HARICOTS VERTS

NIÇOISE SALAD WITH HARICOTS VERTS & YUKON GOLD POTATOES

Tender green beans; tiny, buttery potatoes; and salty capers and olives are the highlights of this Niçoise salad. Try to use good-quality, oil-packed canned tuna to add another layer of flavor. Anchovies and hard-cooked eggs have been omitted to keep the dish light, but feel free to add them. If you have any fingerling potatoes on hand, substitute them for the Yukon Golds, or use leftovers from any of our Fingerling Potato recipes (pp.169–172).

Serves 6 to 8

2 pounds baby Yukon Gold potatoes, halved (or large Yukon Gold potatoes, cut into 1-inch pieces)

Kosher salt

1 pound haricots verts, trimmed and cut in half

3 tablespoons red-wine vinegar

1 tablespoon whole-grain Dijon mustard

¾ cup extra-virgin olive oil

1 medium shallot, finely diced (about 3 tablespoons)

1 tablespoon chopped fresh thyme

Freshly ground black pepper

1 can tuna (12 ounces, preferably oil-packed), drained well and flaked

2 tablespoons capers, rinsed and drained

1 pint cherry tomatoes, halved

¾ cup pitted Niçoise or Kalamata olives, coarsely chopped

Set the potatoes in a large (6-quart) pot, cover them with cold water by a couple of inches, stir in 2 tablespoons salt, and bring to a boil. Reduce the heat to a gentle simmer, cover, and cook until the potatoes are tender when pierced with a fork, about 10 to 12 minutes. Stir in the haricots verts and cook until they turn bright green and tender, about 3 to 4 minutes. Drain well and cool under running water.

In a blender or food processor, blend the vinegar with the mustard. With the machine still running, add the oil in a slow, steady stream so the mixture comes together into a thick emulsion. Add the shallot, 2 teaspoons thyme, 1 teaspoon salt, and 1 teaspoon pepper, and purée until incorporated. Taste and season the dressing with more

continued

TRIMMING GREEN BEANS

These small beans are more delicate than green beans, but you'll still want to trim the ends. It's slow to snap off the stems by hand; instead, grab a small handful of the beans, line up the stem ends, and trim them as a group with a chef's knife.

prep this

salt and pepper if needed. Add 1 or 2 tablespoons water if needed to thin the dressing to a pourable consistency. Transfer the potatoes and beans to a large mixing bowl and toss well with half the vinaigrette. Taste and season with salt and pepper if needed and transfer to a large platter. In the same mixing bowl, toss the tuna with the capers and 2 or 3 tablespoons of the vinaigrette, and set them over the potatoes in the center of the platter. Sprinkle the tomatoes and olives over the potatoes, around the perimeter of the tuna. Drizzle the salad with the remaining vinaigrette, sprinkle with the remaining 1 teaspoon thyme, and serve.

To plate individually, lightly toss the potatoes, beans, tomatoes, and olives with half the vinaigrette and plate; top with the tuna, capers, and the remaining thyme; and serve the remaining dressing on the side.

left: niçoise salad with **haricots verts** & Yukon Gold potatoes

ITALIAN GREEN BEANS
WITH TOMATOES & BALSAMIC

This is a speedy version of slow-cooked Italian green beans, elegant in its simplicity. Sauté the haricots verts quickly to preserve their delicate texture, then toss them with a sauce of plum tomatoes and balsamic vinegar.

Serves 6

Kosher salt

¾ pound haricots verts, trimmed

2 tablespoons olive oil

2 medium cloves garlic, smashed

2 large plum tomatoes, roughly chopped
   and puréed in a food processor

1 tablespoon balsamic vinegar

Freshly ground black pepper

Shavings of Parmigiano-Reggiano,
   for garnish (optional)

Bring a pot of well-salted water to a boil. Add the beans and cook until bright green and just tender, 3 to 4 minutes. Drain and immediately plunge in a large bowl of ice water. Let cool for 3 to 4 minutes. Drain and set aside.

Heat the oil in a large (12-inch) skillet over medium heat. Add the garlic and cook for about 1 minute. Add the tomatoes and vinegar, sprinkle with ½ teaspoon each salt and pepper, and cook, stirring until the mixture reduces by half, about 2 minutes. Add the beans to the pan and cook until warmed through and coated with the tomato mixture, about 1 minute. Taste the beans and season with salt and pepper if needed; garnish with shavings of Parmigiano-Reggiano if desired. Serve immediately.

STIR-FRIED GREEN BEANS WITH GINGER & BLACK BEAN SAUCE

Though these delicate green beans are traditionally saved for fancy French preparations, they're also perfect for a quick stir-fry. Jarred black bean sauce serves as a light base for the sauce while minced ginger and garlic impart a heady punch.

Serves 4

1 tablespoon reduced-sodium soy sauce

2 tablespoons Chinese black bean sauce (like Lee Kum Kee™)

1 tablespoon rice vinegar

2 teaspoons Asian sesame oil

1 teaspoon granulated sugar

3 tablespoons canola oil

1 pound haricots verts, trimmed

Kosher salt

2 tablespoons minced ginger

1 medium clove garlic, minced

In a small bowl, mix the soy sauce, black bean sauce, vinegar, sesame oil, and sugar, and set aside. Heat the canola oil in a large (12-inch) straight-sided sauté pan over medium-high heat until shimmering. Add the beans, sprinkle with ¼ teaspoon salt, and cook, tossing occasionally, until most of the beans are browned, shrunken, and tender, 8 to 10 minutes. Reduce the heat to low and add the ginger and garlic; cook for about 45 seconds.

Add the soy sauce mixture to the pan, cook for another 30 seconds, until the beans are coated and the sauce is warmed through, and serve.

MAKE IT LAST These tender green beans hold quite nicely in the refrigerator in a zip-top bag for one week. Wash them as you go. For long-term storage, rinse and cut the beans to size, trimming the ends, and then blanch them. Let them drain and then freeze in a single layer on a baking sheet so individual beans don't clump together; transfer to zip-top bags or airtight containers in the freezer, where they'll keep for at least six months.

BLUEBERRIES

Nothing is more quintessentially summer than sun-ripened blueberries. Tart and sweet, firm and juicy, these fruits are the treasure of the season that should be savored by the handful.

BLUEBERRY
CHEESECAKE WITH
GINGERSNAP CRUST

Blueberries contrast nicely the richness of this cheesecake and pair perfectly with the gingersnap crust. The cheesecake needs to chill for about 8 hours in the refrigerator, so you may want to make it a day ahead.

Serves 8 to 10

FOR THE CRUST

2 cups ground gingersnap cookies (about 35 cookies)

3 ounces (6 tablespoons) unsalted butter, melted, more for the pan

2 tablespoons granulated sugar

FOR THE FILLING & TOPPING

1½ pounds blueberries (about 4 cups), rinsed, dried, and picked through

1½ cups granulated sugar

Finely grated zest and juice of 1 lemon

¼ teaspoon freshly grated nutmeg

2 teaspoons cornstarch

Three 8-ounce packages cream cheese, softened

1 cup sour cream (not low- or nonfat)

2 large eggs

2 large egg yolks

1 teaspoon pure vanilla extract

Position a rack in the center of the oven and heat the oven to 350°F. Butter a 9-inch springform pan.

PREPARE & BAKE THE CRUST

In a medium bowl, toss the gingersnap crumbs with the melted butter and sugar. Pour the crumbs into the prepared pan and, using your fingers and the bottom of a flat glass, tamp down the crust so it's even on the bottom and goes about an inch up the sides of the pan. Bake the crust until it browns lightly and puffs slightly, 10 to 15 minutes. Transfer to a rack to cool to room temperature.

MAKE THE FILLING

Combine the blueberries, ½ cup of the sugar, the lemon zest and juice, and nutmeg in a large (12-inch) sauté pan and let sit for 5 minutes so the blueberries start to release their juices. Cook over medium-high heat, shaking the pan, until the blueberries start to soften and their juices boil, 3 to 4 minutes. Whisk the cornstarch with 2 tablespoons water and stir into the blueberry mixture so it thickens. Remove from the heat and let cool to room temperature.

continued

MACERATING BLUEBERRIES

Blueberries alone are delicious, but there is always room for a little extra flavor. Sprinkle a bowlful of berries generously with sugar, and then add a splash of liqueur (like Grand Marnier®) and some freshly squeezed lemon juice. The sugar and lemon juice will start to break down the blueberries, pulling out their juices so all the flavors marry, making them the perfect accompaniment for yogurt or vanilla ice cream.

Transfer 1½ cups of this mixture to a blender and purée. Strain the puréed mixture through a fine mesh sieve, discard the solids, and reserve the liquid. Put the remaining blueberries in an airtight container in the refrigerator.

Beat the cream cheese and the remaining 1 cup sugar in a stand mixer with the paddle attachment (or in a large bowl with electric beaters) on medium speed until the mixture is well combined (you may need to use a spatula to free the paddle of the cheese). Reduce to low speed and, one at a time, add the sour cream, eggs, egg yolks, puréed blueberry mixture, and vanilla, and beat until just incorporated. Pour the batter into the gingersnap crust. Wrap the bottom and sides of the springform pan in aluminum foil, making sure the foil goes about three-quarters up the sides of the pan, and then put the springform pan in a large roasting pan. Pour hot water into the roasting pan so it reaches about halfway up the sides of the springform pan (the foil will prevent water from seeping into the pan).

Carefully transfer the roasting pan to the oven and bake until the top of the cake sets but the center still jiggles slightly when shaken, about 1 hour. Using a metal spatula and an oven mitt, carefully remove the springform pan from the water bath, discard the foil, and transfer to a cooling rack to cool to room temperature, about 1 hour. Refrigerate the cake uncovered until completely chilled, about 8 hours. Run a paring knife along the sides of the cake to separate it from the pan and then unlatch and remove the sides of the springform pan. Use a metal spatula to loosen the bottom crust from the pan, and then, using two spatulas, transfer the cake to a serving plate. Spoon the refrigerated blueberries on top of the cake. Cut into slices and serve.

MAKE IT LAST If you plan to eat blueberries within a day or two after getting them home, you can leave them uncovered at room temperature. For longer storage, refrigerate them in a zip-top bag. Rinse the berries as you eat them, not all at once, to prevent mold from appearing. To freeze blueberries, rinse and thoroughly dry them, then freeze them on a baking sheet in a single layer (this prevents the berries from freezing together in one large mass). After the berries are frozen, pack them in airtight containers or zip-top bags.

left: **blueberry cheesecake** with gingersnap crust

PEACH & BLUEBERRY GALETTE

This rustic fruit tart is the perfect vehicle for ripe summer blueberries and peaches. The crust is free form—it just gets folded over the filling and then baked. Serve warm with a scoop of vanilla ice cream or a dollop of crème fraîche.

Serves 8 to 10

FOR THE CRUST

6¾ ounces (1½ cups) unbleached all-purpose flour, more for rolling

1 tablespoon granulated sugar

½ teaspoon table salt

5½ ounces (11 tablespoons) unsalted butter, chilled and cut into ½-inch dice

1 large egg yolk

3 tablespoons whole milk

FOR THE FILLING

1 pound peaches, peeled and cut into ½-inch slices (about 2 cups)

¾ pound blueberries, rinsed and picked through (about 2 cups)

¼ cup light muscovado sugar or light brown sugar

2 tablespoons unbleached all-purpose flour

¼ teaspoon ground cinnamon

Pinch of table salt

1 large egg, beaten

2 tablespoons demerara sugar

MAKE THE DOUGH

Combine the flour, sugar, and salt in a stand mixer fitted with a paddle attachment at low speed. Add the butter to the flour. Mix until the flour is no longer white and holds together when you clump it with your fingers, 1 to 2 minutes. If there are still lumps of butter larger than the size of peas, break them up with your fingers.

In a small bowl, beat the egg yolk and milk, and add to the flour mixture. Mix on low speed just until the dough comes together, about 15 seconds; the dough will be somewhat soft. Turn the dough out onto a sheet of plastic wrap, press it into a flat disk, wrap it in the plastic, and let it rest in the refrigerator for 15 to 20 minutes before rolling out. Meanwhile, position a rack in the center of the oven and heat the oven to 350°F. Line a large rimmed baking sheet with parchment paper.

MAKE THE FILLING & ROLL OUT THE DOUGH

In a medium bowl, toss the peaches and blueberries with the muscovado sugar, flour, cinnamon, and salt.

Lightly flour a large work surface and roll out the dough to a 12- to 13-inch round. Transfer to the prepared baking sheet. Arrange the fruit in the center of the dough, leaving about 1½ inches of space around the perimeter of the dough empty. Fold the outside edge of the dough over the fruit, making occasional pleats. Brush the crust

with the egg. Sprinkle the demerara sugar evenly over the dough and fruit.

Bake the galette until the crust turns a light brown and the filling bubbles, about 50 minutes. Let cool for 10 minutes then cut into wedges and serve warm.

CORNMEAL BLUEBERRY PANCAKES WITH SPICED MAPLE BUTTER

While cornmeal gives these pancakes a hearty texture and blueberries offer a fresh tartness, the spicy sweet butter puts them over the top. Add warmed maple syrup for a little more sweetness.

Serves 4 to 6

FOR THE MAPLE BUTTER
4 ounces (½ cup) unsalted butter, softened
¼ cup pure maple syrup
Kosher salt
¼ teaspoon chili powder
¼ teaspoon ground cinnamon

FOR THE PANCAKES
7¾ ounces (1¾ cups) unbleached
   all-purpose flour
¾ cup yellow cornmeal
1 tablespoon granulated sugar
2 teaspoons baking powder
½ teaspoon baking soda
½ teaspoon table salt
2¼ cups buttermilk
¼ cup vegetable oil
3 large eggs
1 teaspoon pure vanilla extract
1 pint blueberries (¾ pound),
   rinsed and picked through
Unsalted butter, for cooking

MAKE THE MAPLE BUTTER
Put all the ingredients in a food processor and process, scraping down the sides of the bowl if necessary, until the mixture becomes smooth and uniform. Transfer to a large piece of plastic wrap, wrap it, roll it into a log and secure the ends as if it were a sausage. Refrigerate for at least an hour to a couple of days before serving.

MAKE THE PANCAKES
In a large bowl, mix together the flour, cornmeal, sugar, baking powder, baking soda, and salt. In a medium bowl, whisk the buttermilk with the oil, eggs, and vanilla. Gently whisk the buttermilk mixture into the flour mixture until it's mostly uniform (a few lumps are fine).

Heat a large stovetop griddle or large (12-inch) heavy-duty pan (like a cast-iron skillet) over medium heat until a droplet of water immediately evaporates upon hitting the pan. Melt a small pat of butter in the pan, pour in the batter (about ⅓ cup for each pancake), and then sprinkle with the blueberries. Leave space between each pancake so flipping them isn't a problem. Cook the pancakes until bubbles form on top, the cakes set around the edges, and the bottoms brown, about 2 to 3 minutes. Flip and cook on the other side until they brown and the cakes become just firm to the touch, about 2 more minutes. Serve immediately topped with a pat of the maple butter.

FINGERLING POTATOES

These little potatoes aren't always easy to find. So when you see them, don't hesitate. Varying in color and shape, fingerlings will surprise you again and again.

SMASHED FINGERLING POTATOES
WITH RED-WINE VINEGAR & CHIVES

This dish—a cross between mashed potatoes and a warm potato salad—is proof that fingerling potatoes need little adornment. Good olive oil, red-wine vinegar, and thinly sliced chives do the trick. As with German potato salads, the potatoes are tossed with the vinegar while they're still hot so that they absorb the tangy flavor.

Serves 6

2 pounds fingerling potatoes, cut into 1-inch pieces
Kosher salt
2 tablespoons red-wine vinegar
Freshly ground black pepper
⅓ cup extra-virgin olive oil
½ cup thinly sliced chives

Put the potatoes in a medium pot, cover with cold water by a couple of inches, stir in 1 tablespoon salt, and bring to a boil. Reduce to a simmer, cover, and cook until the potatoes are completely tender when pierced with a fork, 10 to 15 minutes. Drain well and transfer to a large mixing bowl. Drizzle with the vinegar and 1 teaspoon pepper; gently smash (not quite mashing) and toss the potatoes with a large fork. Once the potatoes have absorbed all of the vinegar, drizzle the oil over the potatoes and gently smash and toss the potatoes again so that they absorb all of the oil. Fold in the chives, taste, and season with salt and pepper if needed.

ROASTED FINGERLING POTATO CRISPS
WITH SHALLOTS & ROSEMARY

Try to cut the fingerlings no larger than 1/8 inch thick, so that the potatoes will crisp in the oven. (Using a mandolin will allow you to cut them even thinner.) These crisps make a great accompaniment to grilled steak or roasted fish.

Serves 4

1 pound fingerling potatoes, thinly sliced lengthwise (about 1/8-inch thick)

3 tablespoons olive oil

2 large shallots, sliced 1/4-inch thick and broken into individual rings

2 teaspoons chopped fresh rosemary

Kosher salt and freshly ground black pepper

Position a rack in the center of the oven and heat the oven to 425°F. Line a large, rimmed baking sheet with parchment paper or aluminum foil.

In a large bowl, toss the potato slices with the oil, shallots, rosemary, 1 1/4 teaspoons salt, and 1/2 teaspoon pepper, and then spread the chips flat on the baking sheet. Bake the potatoes, turning after 10 minutes, until they brown and start to crisp, 25 to 30 minutes; the shallots should be tender and browned. Serve immediately.

PETITE POTATOES

Like heirloom tomatoes, fingerling potatoes are an old variety that has been resuscitated by the advent of farmers' markets and organic growers. They get their name from their small, finger-length size and come in a range of colors, from white, yellow, and orange to red and purple. The Russian banana, the most common fingerling variety, has yellow flesh and a buttery texture similar to that of Yukon Gold. Fingerlings are delicious sliced and roasted, pan-fried, or mashed with butter and fresh herbs.

PAN-FRIED SOUTHWESTERN HASH

Buttery fingerling potatoes and a healthy punch of spice wake up your basic breakfast hash. This technique—parboiling the potatoes and then sautéing them and the onions and peppers separately—ensures that the potatoes have a soft interior and crisp exterior.

Serves 4 to 6

1¼ pounds fingerling potatoes, cut into ½-inch pieces

Kosher salt

⅓ cup canola oil

1 large yellow onion, finely diced (about 1 cup)

½ large red bell pepper, cut into ¼-inch dice (about ¾ cup)

½ medium green bell pepper, cut into ¼-inch dice (about ½ cup)

1 teaspoon chili powder

1 teaspoon fresh oregano

Freshly ground black pepper

Put the potatoes in a 3-quart saucepan, cover with cold water by a couple of inches, stir in 1 tablespoon salt, and bring to a boil. Reduce to a simmer, cover, and cook until the potatoes are tender but still firm, about 10 minutes. Drain well.

Heat 3 tablespoons oil in a large (12-inch), heavy-duty skillet over medium-high heat until shimmering. Lower the heat to medium, add the potatoes, sprinkle with ¼ teaspoon salt, and cook, stirring occasionally, until they brown and start to crisp, 6 to 8 minutes. Transfer to a large plate.

Raise the heat to medium high, pour the remaining oil into the skillet, add the onion and bell peppers, sprinkle with ½ teaspoon salt, and cook, tossing occasionally, until they brown and become somewhat tender, about 4 minutes. Stir in the chili powder, oregano, and ½ teaspoon pepper, and cook, tossing, for 30 seconds so the spices become fragrant. Add the potatoes and cook, tossing, until they heat through and pick up the flavors of the vegetables and spices, about 2 minutes. Taste and season with salt and pepper if needed, then serve.

MAKE IT LAST Store fingerling potatoes like any other potato: in a cool, dark place away from sunlight. Avoid putting them in the refrigerator, as moisture causes the spuds to sprout. Be mindful that fingerlings will not typically keep as long as full-size potatoes so check them regularly and immediately discard any that give off an odor or have soft spots.

With a sweet crunch and vibrant color, sugar snap peas are great eaten raw as a snack or tossed into a quick stir-fry. As the French say—*mange tout*—you can eat them pod and all.

SUGAR
SNAP PEAS

HOISIN SNAP PEA & CARROT SALAD

Hoisin sauce is a Chinese dipping sauce that is often used with barbecued meats and in stir-fries. Salty, sweet, and spicy, hoisin sauce gives this simple side of snap peas and carrots distinctive flavor. The taste of the sauce can be strong; feel free to dilute it with a tablespoon of water or more depending on personal preference.

Serves 6

2 tablespoons hoisin sauce

1 tablespoon reduced-sodium soy sauce

1 tablespoon rice vinegar

2 teaspoons Asian sesame oil

3 tablespoons canola oil

10 ounces sugar snap peas, ends trimmed

3 medium carrots, peeled and thinly sliced on the diagonal (about 2 cups)

1 small red onion, thinly sliced

Kosher salt

1 tablespoon minced ginger

In a small bowl, mix together the hoisin sauce, soy sauce, vinegar, and sesame oil.

Heat the canola oil in a medium (10-inch), heavy-duty skillet over medium-high heat until shimmering. Add the vegetables, sprinkle with ½ teaspoon salt, and cook, stirring, until the vegetables brown in places and start to soften, about 4 minutes. Add the ginger and cook for another 30 seconds. Add ½ cup water and cook, tossing, until the vegetables are crisp-tender and the water mostly cooks off, about 4 minutes. Toss with the hoisin mixture, then transfer to a large bowl and serve.

TRIMMING SNAP PEAS

Though it's perfectly fine to eat snap peas without trimming the strings that run from end to end, you'll have a far nicer dining experience without them. To remove them, pinch off the stem and then, grasping the stringy seam between your thumb and a knife blade, pull it away.

prep this

SAUTÉED SUGAR SNAP PEAS
WITH MUSHROOMS & BACON

With the addition of bacon and mushrooms, this dish is quite substantial and filling. It is a perfect side for a Sunday dinner of roast lamb or roast beef.

Serves 4 to 6

3 slices thickly sliced bacon, cut into strips

3 cloves garlic, smashed

2 tablespoons olive oil

3/4 pound sugar snap peas, ends trimmed

Kosher salt

10 ounces small white mushrooms, halved (or large white mushrooms, quartered)

1/3 cup dry sherry

1 teaspoon sherry vinegar

1 1/2 tablespoons coarsely chopped fresh tarragon

In a large (12-inch) skillet over medium heat, cook the bacon and garlic with 1 tablespoon oil until the bacon lightly browns and renders most of its fat, about 6 minutes. Transfer the bacon to a plate lined with paper towels; let it drain and cool, and then crumble it. Discard the garlic from the skillet.

Raise the heat to medium high; add the snap peas, sprinkle with 3/4 teaspoon salt, and cook, stirring, until they turn bright green and start to brown in places, about 2 minutes. Transfer the peas to a plate.

Add the remaining tablespoon oil and the mushrooms to the pan, sprinkle with 1/2 teaspoon salt, and cook, stirring, until the mushrooms brown and start to soften, about 5 minutes. Add the sherry and cook, stirring, until the liquid almost completely reduces, about 2 minutes. Return the snap peas to the skillet, drizzle in the sherry vinegar, and cook, tossing, for 1 minute. Transfer to a serving dish, toss with the tarragon, and sprinkle with the bacon just before serving.

MAKE IT LAST Snap peas tend to have a long shelf life. They should hold for at least one week in a zip-top bag in the crisper drawer of the refrigerator. Freezing fresh snap pea pods is also an option. Blanch them in boiling water for 2 to 3 minutes, then immediately plunge them in cool water, and drain. Freeze them in a single layer on a baking sheet to prevent them from sticking together in a frozen clump. Once frozen, pack them in airtight containers or zip-top bags and put them in the freezer.

SESAME BEEF & SNAP PEAS

A drizzle of chili sauce gives the tangy sauce in this dish a touch of heat while toasted sesame seeds and sesame oil offer a double shot of flavor. Served with steamed rice, this dish comes together in minutes for a quick weekday meal.

Serves 4

1 pound flank steak or skirt steak, cut into thin strips

1 tablespoon plus 1 teaspoon reduced-sodium soy sauce

1 tablespoon plus 1 teaspoon Asian sesame oil

Kosher salt

1 tablespoon ketchup

2 teaspoons rice vinegar

1 teaspoon granulated sugar

1 teaspoon Asian chili sauce (like Sriracha)

2 teaspoons sesame seeds, toasted (see Toasting Nuts, p. 41)

3 tablespoons canola or peanut oil

3 tablespoons finely chopped ginger

10 ounces sugar snap peas, ends trimmed

1 teaspoon cornstarch

Toss the beef with 1 teaspoon each of soy sauce and sesame oil and ¼ teaspoon salt. In a small bowl, mix the remaining tablespoon each of soy sauce and sesame oil with the ketchup, vinegar, sugar, chili sauce, and half of the sesame seeds.

Heat 1½ tablespoons oil in a large (12-inch) skillet or wok over medium-high heat until shimmering. Add the beef and cook, stirring occasionally, until it loses its raw color and browns in places, about 2 to 3 minutes. Transfer to a large plate. Cook the ginger with the remaining 1½ tablespoons oil until it sizzles steadily and starts to brown lightly around the edges, about 1 minute. Add the snap peas, sprinkle with ¼ teaspoon salt, and cook, stirring, until they turn bright green and start to brown in places, 1 to 2 minutes. Add ⅓ cup water and cook, stirring, until about half of the liquid cooks off and the peas start to soften, about 1 minute. Add the soy sauce mixture and beef, and cook, stirring, for a couple minutes until the mixture heats through and coats the peas and beef. Whisk the cornstarch with ¼ cup water; add to the beef, and cook, stirring, until the sauce thickens, about 1 minute. Sprinkle with the remaining teaspoon sesame seeds, and serve.

MANGOS

Juicy, fragrant, and sweet, the mango is one exotic fruit that you'll want to become fast friends with. It's hard to eat just one, so buy them in bulk when you get the chance.

TROPICAL MANGO SORBET

Papaya and pineapple juice build on the clean, sweet flavor of mango in this sorbet, while a splash of coconut milk smoothes its texture. If papayas aren't readily available or in season, just add another mango.

Serves 6

4 mangos (about 3 pounds), pitted and cut into ½-inch dice (about 4 cups)

1 medium papaya (about ¾ pound), cut into ½-inch dice (about 1½ cups)

1 cup pineapple juice

½ cup granulated sugar

¼ cup coconut milk

Finely grated zest and juice of 1 lime

Working in batches if necessary, purée all of the ingredients in a blender until smooth. Transfer the mixture to a bowl, cover, and refrigerate until cold (about 2 hours). Freeze in an ice-cream machine according to the manufacturer's instructions. Transfer the sorbet to an airtight container and freeze overnight to finish setting. Take the sorbet out of the freezer and let it soften for about 5 minutes before serving. It will keep in the freezer for about two weeks.

PITTING MANGOS

To remove a mango pit, position the mango upright and cut downward using a chef's knife, parallel to the pit but slightly off center. If you feel resistance, that's the pit; move the knife farther from the center and make the slice again. Do the same for the other side, cutting downward away from the center; discard the pit. Score the flesh of the fruit almost all the way to the skin lengthwise and then widthwise in the desired dice size. Use a spoon to scoop out the diced mango.

prep this

ISLAND-SPICED CHICKEN SALAD WITH MANGO & SCALLIONS

This sweet and spicy salad is the perfect meal on a warm summer night.
Serve in Boston lettuce leaf cups. This recipe makes plenty; put any
leftovers on top of greens or in a tortilla for an easy lunch.

Serves 6

Kosher salt and freshly ground
  black pepper
1/2 teaspoon ground allspice
1/2 teaspoon ground cinnamon
Heaping 1/4 teaspoon chipotle powder
2 pounds boneless, skinless chicken thighs
  (about 8), trimmed of fatty patches
2 Anaheim or poblano chiles, halved,
  cored, and seeded
6 scallions (both white and green parts),
  ends trimmed
3 tablespoons canola or peanut oil
2 mangos (about 1 1/2 pounds), pitted
  and cut into 1/2-inch dice (about 2 cups)
1 tablespoon fresh lime juice,
  more to taste

For a gas grill, light the front burner to medium-high and the back burner(s) to medium. For a charcoal grill, light a medium-high fire (400°F) with two-thirds of the coals banked to one side. Clean and oil the grill grates.

In a small bowl, mix 1 1/2 teaspoons salt and 1 teaspoon pepper with the allspice, cinnamon, and chipotle powder. Sprinkle the chicken all over with the spice rub. Sprinkle the chiles and scallions with 1 tablespoon oil, 1/2 teaspoon salt, and 1/2 teaspoon pepper.

Set the chicken over the hot zone of the fire, and the chiles and scallions over the cooler zone. Grill until the chicken, peppers, and scallions have good grill marks, 3 to 4 minutes. Continue to grill the peppers and scallions until they brown and become just tender, about 3 minutes more. Grill the chicken, flipping as needed, until it is firm to the touch and cooked through (slice into a thicker piece of the chicken with a knife to check), 6 to 8 more minutes. Transfer the chicken and vegetables to a large cutting board to cool. Coarsely chop the chicken, peppers, and scallions.

In a large serving bowl, toss the mango with the chicken, peppers, and scallions. Add the lime juice and the remaining 2 tablespoons oil and toss well. Season with more lime juice, salt, and pepper if needed. Serve immediately.

MAKE IT LAST Store mangos at room temperature until they become just soft and ripe, and then transfer to the refrigerator where they'll keep for up to one week. To ripen the fruit more quickly, store in a paper bag at room temperature. Mangos can also be sliced and the fruit frozen whole or as a purée.

SPICY MANGO SALSA

This tangy salsa's heat comes from fiery habaneros, available in most supermarkets; if you can't find them, go with jalapeños instead. When working with the chiles, it is a good idea to wear gloves, or wash your hands and knife thoroughly after touching them. The bright color and sweetness of the mango in the salsa isn't overpowered by the onion and red pepper, which are quickly seared over high heat to mellow their flavor and texture. The salsa goes great with grilled chicken, steaks, or a full-flavored fish like salmon or tuna.

Serves 6; makes about 3 cups

¼ canola oil

½ medium red onion, finely diced (about ½ cup)

1 medium red bell pepper, cut into ¼-inch dice (about 1¼ cups)

Kosher salt

2 mangos (about 1½ pounds), pitted and cut into ½-inch dice (about 2 cups)

¼ cup chopped fresh cilantro

1 habanero (or 1 to 2 jalapeños), stemmed, seeded, and very finely diced (about 1 tablespoon)

2 tablespoons fresh lime juice

Heat the oil in a medium (10-inch) skillet over medium-high heat until shimmering. Add the onion and red pepper; sprinkle with 1 teaspoon salt, and cook, stirring, until the vegetables just start to brown and soften a bit, 2 to 3 minutes. Transfer to a large plate to cool. Once cool, transfer to a medium bowl and toss with the mangos, cilantro, habanero, and 1 table-spoon lime juice. Season the salsa with the remaining tablespoon of lime juice and salt if needed, and serve.

EQUIVALENCY CHARTS

LIQUID/DRY MEASURES

U.S.	Metric
¼ teaspoon	1.25 milliliters
½ teaspoon	2.5 milliliters
1 teaspoon	5 milliliters
1 tablespoon (3 teaspoons)	15 milliliters
1 fluid ounce (2 tablespoons)	30 milliliters
¼ cup	60 milliliters
⅓ cup	80 milliliters
½ cup	120 milliliters
1 cup	240 milliliters
1 pint (2 cups)	480 milliliters
1 quart (4 cups, 32 ounces)	960 milliliters
1 gallon (4 quarts)	3.84 liters
1 ounce (by weight)	28 grams
1 pound	454 grams
2.2 pounds	1 kilogram

OVEN TEMPERATURES

°F	Gas Mark	°C
250	½	120
275	1	140
300	2	150
325	3	165
350	4	180
375	5	190
400	6	200
425	7	220
450	8	230
475	9	240
500	10	260
550	Broil	290

INDEX